DISCOVER

DRIED FLOWERS

DISCOVER
DRIED FLOWERS

40 ORIGINAL PROJECTS TO BUILD YOUR FLOWER-ARRANGING SKILLS

CHRISTOPHER HAMMOND

HAMLYN

First published in Great Britain in 1994 by Hamlyn
an imprint of Reed Consumer Books Limited,
Michelin House, 81 Fulham Road, London SW3 6RB
and Auckland, Melbourne, Singapore and Toronto

SERIES EDITOR: **JONATHAN HILTON**
SERIES ART EDITOR: **PRUE BUCKNELL**
ART EDITOR: **ALISON SHACKLETON**
EXECUTIVE EDITOR: **JUDITH MORE**
ART DIRECTOR: **JACQUI SMALL**

PHOTOGRAPHS BY: **LUCY MASON**

The publishers have made every effort to ensure that all instructions given in this book are accurate and safe, but they cannot accept liability for any resulting injury, damage or loss to either person or property whether direct or consequential and howsoever arising. The author and publishers will be grateful for any information which will assist them in keeping future editions up to date.

ISBN: 0 60058 302 3

DTP ALISON SHACKLETON
ORIGINATION BY MANDARIN, SINGAPORE
PRINTED AND BOUND IN BARCELONA, SPAIN BY CAYFOSA

CONTENTS

INTRODUCTION

Although we may appreciate fresh flowers in the home, often there simply is not time to buy, arrange, renew, water and maintain them on a regular basis. With a dried flower arrangement, your initial investment of time, effort and imagination will be repaid not just over a period of many weeks or months but, with the minimum of attention and a little refurbishment, your arrangement could go on giving you pleasure over a period of years.

The trick with flower arranging, as with any new skill, is to start slowly. If you make mistakes, or are not happy with a finished piece, it doesn't matter – in nearly all cases you can dismantle what you have done with absolutely no harm to the flowers and just start again.

The projects you will find in this book have been designed to illustrate the different techniques and concepts involved in dried flower arranging. They will show you how to put these ideas into practice, to explore the use of colour and texture, and to stimulate your imagination. To make the practical side simpler, each arrangement is shown as easy-to-follow stages, with detailed photographs taken during the construction of the piece. Once you start, you will rapidly discover the charm and pleasure of this practical and creative hobby.

SHOP-BOUGHT OR HOME-DRIED FLOWERS

All of the materials used for the projects in this book should be readily available at any good florist or dried flower specialist. You may find that the prices asked of some of the exotic or unusual flowers seem high, but bear in mind that if they are treated with a little care they will last for many months, or even years! This may help to put the cost into some perspective, especially when you consider the ever-increasing prices of freshly cut flowers and the scant few days or, at best, weeks they last before fading.

If you have the time and inclination you may want to dry your own fresh flowers, perhaps ones picked from your garden. The simplest method is to hang bunches of flowers upside down and allow the air to circulate freely around them. You will need a place where they can be left undisturbed, such as a cool airing cupboard. A dry garage or garden shed may also be suitable, but not in winter when the air is generally too damp. When arranging flowers in bunches, tie the stems low down so that the heads fall slightly apart and don't bunch together too tightly. Leaves hold moisture longer than the flower heads, so carefully remove excess foliage before hanging.

Grasses, lavender, and others such as dock usually dry better if laid flat on sheets of absorbent paper. Again, arrange the individual stems carefully so that there is plenty of space between the heads for the air to circulate.

If you haven't the free space for either of the methods described above, you can also dry some types of flower standing upright in a vase. Place the stems in about 2in (5cm) of water. The flowers will take up some of the water but most of it will evaporate, leaving the flowers to dry out slowly over a period of weeks. And while they are drying they will still look attractive, giving you an extra bonus. Hydrangea, mimosa and eucalyptus are particularly good subjects for this method.

Another technique involves the use of drying agents. The quickest one to use is silica gel, which will dry plant material in about two days if used in an air-tight container. Make sure that the flower heads are completely covered by the crystals. Borax and fine, dry silver sand mixed together should do the job in about ten days.

Whatever method you use, or if you buy ready dried flowers, I can only hope that this book will encourage you to start exploring your own creative potential.

MATERIALS AND TECHNIQUES

At the start of each project there is a list of materials used in that arrangement, including such things as moss, raffia and various types of dried flowers. Flower names given are, generally, those most commonly used by florists.

Dried flowers normally come in bunches of 10 stems, but this does vary depending on the supplier. As a guide, when making an arrangement you need just one bunch of each flower type, but this does depend on the container size you are using. Before starting, make certain you have sufficient flowers for your intended arrangement and also check that additional flowers can be readily obtained if necessary.

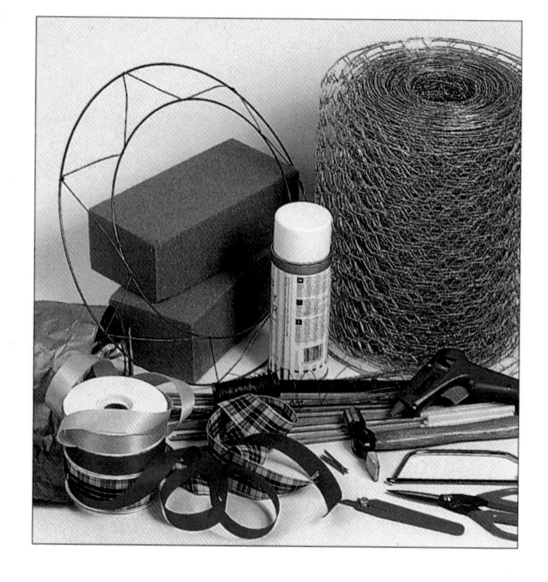

WIRING LOTUS SEED HEADS

Lotus seed heads are often used in arrangements. Take a stub wire and pierce the side of a seed head. Push the wire all the way through and check that an even amount protrudes from either side. Bring both legs down to the pointed end of the seed head and twist the ends of the wire together. The seed head is now ready to be used in an arrangement (*see box opposite*).

GENERAL EQUIPMENT

- Florist's foam for securing flowers
- Chicken wire for making shapes
- Ribbons for bows and decorations
- Canes and wires for fixing and supports
- Hammer, saw, scissors and knife for cutting and fixing
- Ready-made frames for wreaths
- Spray paints for special effects

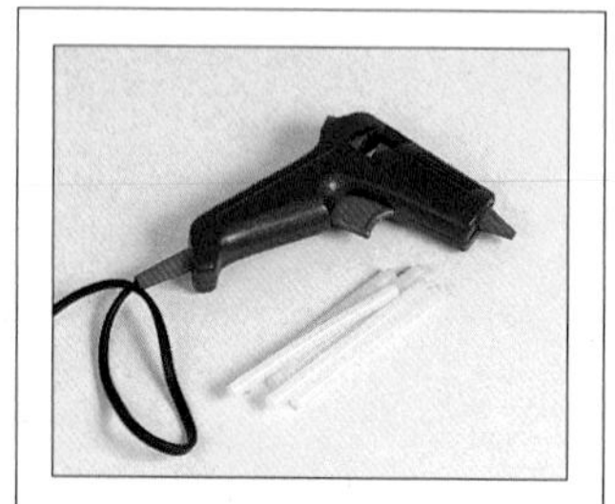

USING A GLUE GUN

You will find a glue gun invaluable, and one has been used in most of the projects in this book, mainly to stick flower heads into position. Stub wires can be used for this purpose, but it takes longer and is very fiddly. When a wire is essential, this is indicated in the text. Take care when using a glue gun since the glue does become very hot. Wipe any off your skin immediately with a damp cloth. Children using one should always be supervised. Threads of glue from the gun may trail over your arrangement. If so, wait for them to dry and carefully pick them off. A hobby glue gun costs about as much to buy as a bunch of dried flowers.

COLOUR HARMONY AND CONTRAST

Choice of flower and foliage colour is crucial in setting the right mood. You can be bold here, opting for strong colour contrasts or go for subtle shadings within a more restricted colour range, such as the blue of the larkspur and lavender graduating into the blue-pink of the statice. This colour combination forms a link in the flowers seen here (*right*), allowing the vibrant yellow of the thistles to sit in close proximity to the strong red and peach of the roses. After cutting the flower stems to the right size for an arrangement, don't discard the stems. The foliage can often be used as an integral part of a design, providing a strong green that is difficult to find without having to purchase expensive dried or stabilized foliage.

MATERIALS FOR TEXTURE AND STRUCTURE

In many of the arrangements you will see in this book, flowers have been used only as one element of the design. Other materials commonly used, principally for their textural qualities, are pictured here (*right*). Mosses of different types, for example, hessian sacking and natural raffia all seem to have a close affinity with dried flowers, and so they are often used to provide those important finishing touches that help both to show the flowers off to best advantage as well as to disguise the underlying florist's foam, stub wires and so on. Cinnamon sticks are also sometimes used, as are the contorted shapes of willow and strips of bark, and these are all invaluable in giving extra form and structure.

TIPS FOR WIRING

- Wrap a stub wire around the middle of the stems of a bunch of flowers, such as lavender, and twist the ends together making sure to leave them long enough to attach to an arrangement.
- Take care not to crack a lotus seed head when twisting the wire together.
- To wire a pine cone, wrap a long stub wire right around the gap in between the lower tiers of seeds, bring the ends of the wire down and twist them together securely. Make sure to leave the ends of the wire long enough to act as a fixing. The pine cone is now ready to be used in an arrangement.

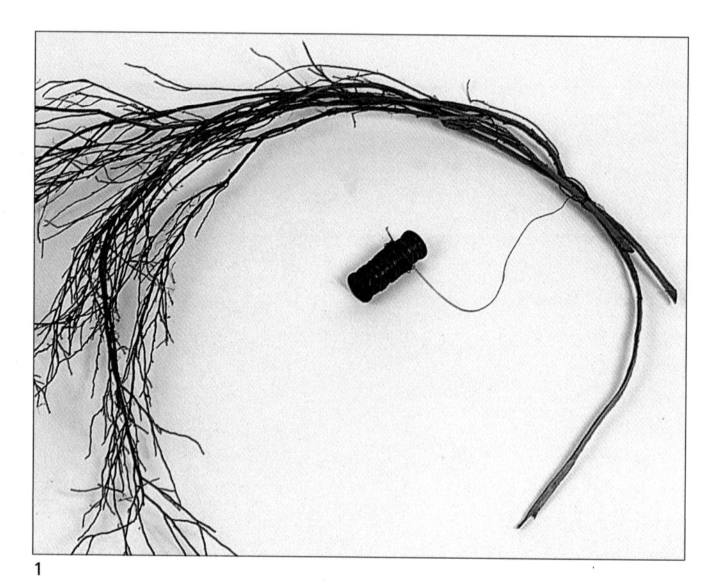

1

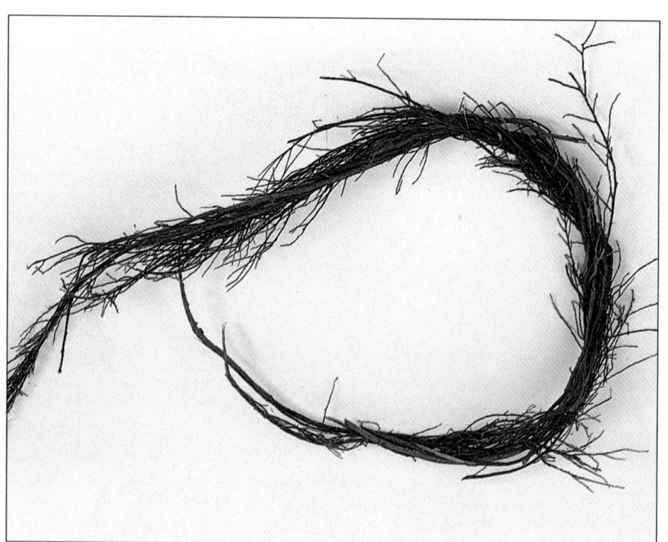

2

3

PREPARING A TWIG WREATH

MATERIALS
Chinese willow branches (other twig wreaths in this book are made from birch)
Reel wire
Scissors

1 Soak your chosen branches in water overnight, or longer if they are really dry. Take a thin branch and gently bend it into a curve. Use only naturally supple branches for wreath making. Wire another curved branch a little way down from the end of the first. Use lengths of thin, strong wire, known as reel wire, to bind the branches together.

2 Bind more and more branches together, elongating the overall curve until you have sufficient to form the size circle you require for your wreath. A wreath can be quite small, as is illustrated in the swagging project (*see pp. 52-5*).

3 Hold the ends of the branches together to form the required size of circle and bind the ends together with reel wire. Tuck the ends underneath into the circle and wind them round the other branches. Form more lengths of branches in the same way and wind them round the circle of branches you have already made. Repeat this until you attain the required thickness for your wreath. Bind all around the wreath with reel wire, securing all the ends, to form a smooth outline. Eventually you can attach the wreath to a wall by making a wire loop secured to the twigs.

WIRE AND MOSS WREATHS OR SHAPES

MATERIALS
Chicken wire
Sphagnum moss
Reel wire
Scissors

1 Making a wreath base to work on out of chicken wire and moss is not difficult, and by using the same technique you can make any base shape you wish. First, cut a length of chicken wire to size. You can cut the width down, too, if necessary, or join widths of chicken wire together if required. Stitch the pieces of chicken wire together with reel wire. Take your chicken wire and start to fill it with handfuls of sphagnum moss.

2 Fill the desired area with sphagnum moss and then roll or bend the chicken wire over to form an outer skin containing the moss inside. Mould the chicken wire into the shape and size you require by firmly squeezing it with both hands.

3 To make a wreath, roll the chicken wire into a sausage shape and then bring the two ends up to meet each other. Stitch the ends together using reel wire. You will need to leave the moss to dry out for about a week (depending on the weather conditions). When the moss has completely dried out, you can fix the wreath to a wall with a wire loop attached to the chicken wire.

1

2

3

TIPS

- For a twig wreath, choose your materials carefully. Branches that are too thick will not happily form a tight curve.
- Branches become pliable if soaked in warm water.
- For a wire wreath or shape, cut away excess chicken wire before shaping.
- Wear thick gloves when shaping chicken wire.

PREPARING A WIRE FRAME WREATH

MATERIALS
Wreath frame
Reel wire
Sphagnum moss
Wire cutters

1 Wire frame wreaths are readily available from dried flower specialists as well as many ordinary florists. To start preparing one for use, secure some reel wire to one of the supporting struts, wrap the wire around the strut and then twist the two ends firmly together.

2 Take handfuls of sphagnum moss and bind them securely on to the wreath frame, again using lengths of reel wire. Methodically work your way around the wreath in this fashion.

3 Once you have covered the frame, you will probably need to go over the shape again, filling in places that look a bit thin with more moss. Don't overfill the frame with moss, however, or bind it too tightly on to the frame, or you may find it impossible to push the stems of your flowers into position. Once you are satisfied with the shape of your wreath, finish by securing the wire to the frame and snip off any exposed ends with the cutters. When the moss has dried out, which may take a week or more, decorate the wreath with your chosen flowers. Attach a wire loop to the frame to act as a hanger.

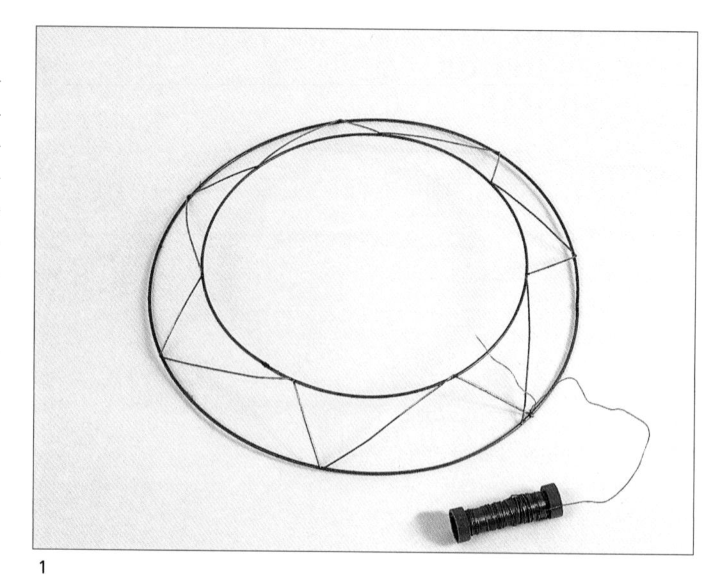

1

2

3

TIPS

- You can obtain wreath frames from florists in many different sizes and shapes.
- If you don't allow the moss to dry out thoroughly, which may take a week or more, trapped moisture will rapidly cause the dried flowers to rot.
- If necessary, heat moss in a barely warm oven to speed up the drying process.

PREPARING A FOAM BLOCK FOR A WALL-MOUNTED ARRANGEMENT

MATERIALS
Florist's foam block
Chicken wire
Reel wire
Wire cutters

1 Take a block of florist's foam and a length of chicken wire, cut so that it is just long enough to wrap around the block. To gauge how long it should be, bend the chicken wire into lengths that correspond to the dimensions of the four sides of the block. Now you will be able to fashion the shape out of chicken wire without actually wrapping it around the foam. If you do wrap the wire around the block to make the shape, you are likely to cut it to pieces. Next, open up the chicken-wire shape and simply slot your block of florist's foam into position.

2 Once you have wrapped the prefolded chicken wire around the block, secure it together with the ends of the cut wire. Lace these over with a pair of cutters or scissors to save your fingers.

3 Now fold in the ends neatly as if wrapping a parcel. Make a wire loop out of reel wire and attach it to the chicken wire ready for hanging on a wall.

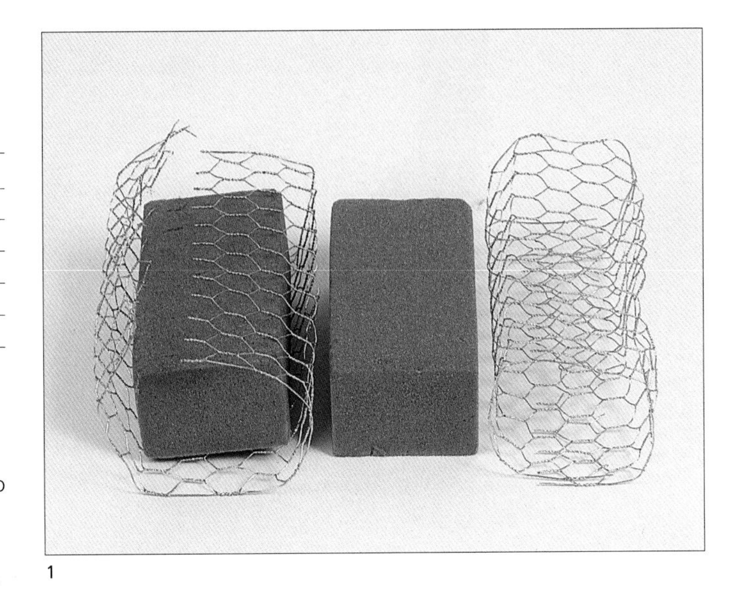

1

2

3

PREPARING A TRUNK AND CONTAINER

MATERIALS

- Tree trunk
- Container
- Plastic bag
- Chicken wire
- Quick-drying cement
- Bucket and water
- Stirring stick
- Scissors
- Moss
- Glue and glue gun

1

2

1 Take your diminutive trunk and place it in a container. Hold it upright with one hand and squash in chicken wire until it stands by itself. Level the trunk by eye not with a spirit level, since it will look false if perfectly straight.

2 Make up some quick-drying cement with water in a container, such as a bucket. Mix it thoroughly with a stick. Once the mixture is ready, pour it into the prepared container with its tree trunk. Be careful not to splash the cement on to the trunk or dribble it on the rim or outside of the container. If your container is, for example, a terracotta flowerpot as pictured here, cover the drainage hole in the bottom with a piece of plastic bag. This will prevent the cement running out before it has had time to harden. The chicken wire will bond with and reinforce the cement. Wait for the cement to dry hard – overnight is preferable – and then glue on moss to cover the surface of the cement.

PREPARING A BASKET

MATERIALS

- Basket
- Florist's foam
- Strong knife
- Scissors
- Stub wire
- Glue and glue gun or other strong adhesive
- Moss

1

2

1 Fill a basket with foam cut to size. Take stub wires, bend them to form hairpin shapes and push them through the weave to secure the foam in place. You may sometimes have to glue the foam to the bottom of the basket for extra strength. For some arrangements the foam will need to stand proud of the rim of the basket so that you can arrange flowers horizontally. Other arrangements will require the surface of the florist's foam to be level with the rim of the basket or container or even a little lower than the rim to leave some room for the addition of moss on top.

2 Now the foam is in place, choose moss to co-ordinate with your arrangement, and sprinkle it over the foam. Bend stub wires into hairpin shapes and push them into the foam to hold the moss in position. Use only the minimum of stub wires to do this; bear in mind that the flower stems of your arrangement piercing the moss will also help to hold it securely. Make sure the moss is not too damp to use for flower arranging. Leave it to dry out a little. Some moss, such as lichen and reindeer moss, will dry to a hard, stiff texture. Use these mosses damp but never wet.

MAKING A BOW

MATERIALS
Ribbon
Scissors

To make a bow, take a length of ribbon in one hand. Your free hand should be your dominant hand. Hold the ribbon with its shiny side toward you between your thumb and first finger. Leave a tail of ribbon that is a little longer than the desired loops of the bow hanging down. Take the ribbon above your thumb and first finger and twist it so the dull side is now facing you. Loop the ribbon around and back into the grip of your thumb and first finger. Ensure that the shiny side of the ribbon comes back over to face you. Gather the ribbon together and twist again so the tail has its dull side to you. Bring the tail in a loop up to meet your thumb and first finger. Bring the shiny side around to face you again and, as you do this, make a loop the same size as the first loop. Imagine a horizontal line crossing between the loops at the point of your finger and thumb. Every even number of loops should stay below this line and every odd number above it. Carry on making loops until the bow is the size you wish. Now cut off the last tail, a little longer than the loops. Tie a length of ribbon along the imaginary horizontal line. Now, using this length of ribbon, secure the bow to the pot, basket or other container you are working on. If you wish, cut V shapes into the tails to finish them off. If texture is your most important consideration, you can make a far simpler bow from strands of raffia, as shown here.

TIPS

- When preparing a basket, use just sufficient moss to cover the foam, not so much that you can't easily push the flower stems through it once it has dried out.

- When making a bow, you can tie a ribbon around an object, leaving the ties long. Place a pre-made bow between the ties and secure it with a knot.

BASKETS

1

2

3

4

5

6

1 Take a prepared basket (*see pp. 10-17*). Cover the florist's foam with gray lichen moss, sometimes known as reindeer moss. Choose your moss covering to co-ordinate with your flowers. It is an integral part of the basket and should be treated as such.

2 Make a circle of sea lavender. Take each sprig and hold it up to the basket to judge how long to cut. Leave sufficient stem that can be pushed well into the foam. Take an uneven number of sprigs and arrange them at right-angles to the foam, so that they come out of the basket horizontally.

3 Fill in with more sprigs of sea lavender arranged throughout the basket. Don't overfill it with lavender, however, since it is acting only as foliage in this design.

4 Use an odd number of roses to create the second wheel of flowers, thus providing an outline for the arrangement.

5 Fill in with the remainder of the roses. Using the rose stems cut into small segments complete with leaves, distribute them as foliage fillers tucked deep into the arrangement.

6 Next, position the blue larkspur in the same way as you did the roses. Cut the larkspur to a slightly longer length than the roses, however, to create more definition. Now place the poppy seed heads deep within the arrangement, scattering them randomly throughout the basket. Fill in any areas that seem a little empty (*see photograph of finished basket opposite*).

MATERIALS
Prepared basket
Sea lavender
Gerdo rose
Blue larkspur
Poppy seed heads
Gray lichen moss

EASY LEVEL

SIMPLE ROUND BASKET

This small, round arrangement is a fine beginning to a chapter on baskets and, being both simple and inexpensive to make, it is an excellent starting point for the beginner. Don't worry if you are not completely happy with your first attempt; carefully remove all the flowers and start afresh.

For this first arrangement, a basket with a heavy weave has been used. The boldness of its structure lends the arrangement visual weight and provides an important contrast with the light, soft textures of the sea lavender and larkspur.

Although this basket has a central handle, don't allow it confuse your arrangement. Create your first "wheel" of flowers as though it were an open basket, not letting it be divided into two separate, front-facing arrangements. A classic combination of pink, white and blue has been used here, producing a pleasing, fresh-looking floral display. The moss here is a gray lichen, which blends well with the colour and texture of the sea lavender.

EASY LEVEL

TROUGH BASKET

Baskets of all shapes and sizes are easy to come across and you should be able to find one suitable for most settings in the home. This trough basket would be perfect somewhere narrow and, since it is also a low arrangement, you could place it on a set of shelves or use it as a centrepiece on a dining table.

One of the most successful aspects of this basket is the length of fabric running through the arrangement. Besides giving interest to the basket, the green damask covers some of the surface area that you would otherwise have to fill with flowers; this cuts down on the costs, especially if you have a suitable remnant of material lying somewhere in a drawer! You may be able to find a piece of the same material that has been used on the soft furnishings in the room the arrangement will stand in.

This basket has a highly textured look to it, created by the use of exotic and unusual flowers. These textured flowers contrast well with the softness and subtlety of the roses and the fluidity of the damask.

MATERIALS
Prepared basket
Stub wires
Banksia coccinea
Orange carthamus
Protea compacta
Cream Success rose
Achillea ptarmica
Green damask

1

2

3

1 Prepare a long, narrow trough basket (*see pp. 10-17*). Take a length of fabric and secure thick stub wires around two diagonal corners. Now position the material to create a fluid, pleasing line. Push the stub wires deep into the florist's foam to secure the fabric.

2 Take three banksia coccinea flowers and cut the stems quite short, about 2-3in (5-7.5cm) below their heads. However, ensure that the stems are long enough to hold the heavy flower heads in position. Group them slightly off-centre, tucking one in under the fabric. Now create a broken snake shape through the basket, from end to end, with the orange carthamus.

3 Next, position four protea compacta in the basket – one group of three at the right-hand corner and one solitary protea at the other end of the basket. Taking in the banksia visually, these form a roughly diagonal line of textured flowers through the arrangement. Fill in with the cream roses, choosing specimens with open blooms, and the achillea ptarmica. Arrange the roses in two main blocks of colour and sprinkle the achillea through them. This will create small areas of coloured highlights. If you still have any gaps in the arrangement, fill them in with more of the carthamus blooms.

1

2

3

4

MATERIALS
Prepared basket
Stub wires
Natural raffia
Green carpet moss
Lavender
Yellow thistles
Sunflowers
Yellow helichrysum
Achillea

1 Prepare a flat, open trug basket (*see pp. 10-17*). Take a bunch of long-stemmed lavender, bind it with natural raffia and tie it in a knot. Leave the ties long. Ensure that the lavender is long enough to overhang the basket in both directions. Secure the horizontal bunch in position with a few stub wires pushed deep into the florist's foam.

2 Take some yellow thistles and cut their stems in half. Take the flowering halves and position them in a pleasing configuration close to the lavender. Arrange the other half of the stems at a corresponding angle in the other side of the foam. To the eye, it should seem that they are lying in one continuous piece. Now repeat this process with the sunflowers. Cut off the thick leaves from the bottom of the stems and use them to surround the sunflower heads.

3 Now take a bunch of bright yellow helichrysum and tie it with a small raffia bow. Take the bunch and secure it with a stub wire into the foam. Position the bunch next to the stem ends of the lavender, allowing the handle to make a natural division through the lavender and helichrysum, separating them and the basket into two different sections.

4 In the remaining part of the basket, arrange the achillea to look as if they, too, are lying sideways. Fill out this last portion of the basket with the large heads of the achillea overhanging the edges.

INTERMEDIATE LEVEL

GROUPED BASKET

At first glance, this basket looks as though somebody has been walking in a beautiful garden at the height of summer, picked bunches of their favourite flowers and laid them in a basket to dry. This is exactly the effect you want to achieve.

In fact, only the lavender and yellow helichrysum are tied in bunches – the others are set in foam to look like bunches. Setting the bottom of the stems into the other side of the foam gives the impression that the stems are continuous. By doing this, you can arrange the flower heads in exactly the position you want – and they will stay put. It also enables you to leave some space around the heads, making the basket seem more abundant than it really is. Use the foliage from the sunflowers by placing the leaves in the foam around the sunflower heads.

The yellow and blue work together extremely well and the green of the carpet moss enhances the foliage of the flowers. A rustic basket has been used to give a country look to the design.

INTERMEDIATE LEVEL

POT-POURRI BASKET

A practical and functional basket can still be a thing of beauty. An example of this is the subject of this project – a pot-pourri basket. By placing dried flowers around the outside, you leave the inside free to be filled with the delicately scented pot-pourri ingredients.

Once you have decided on the contents, you can design the outside so that the flower colours and textures harmonize. In this basket, a mixture of white, blue and red pot-pourri has been used, and this colour scheme is echoed by the white sea lavender, blue larkspur and red roses. The hydrangea heads and scabious flowers both accentuate and reflect the pot-pourri texture.

Select flowers that can be easily bunched and tied, so that you can wire them into place through the weave of the basket. If you wish to use only the flower heads, as with the roses in this arrangement, this will be an opportunity to use a glue gun.

This basket would tantalize the eyes and nose if positioned on a dressing table or on a bathroom shelf.

1

2

3

4

MATERIALS
Basket
Stub wires
Glue and glue gun
Hydrangea heads
Sea lavender
Scabious
Blue larkspur
Mercedes rose
Pot-pourri ingredients

1 Use a dark-coloured rustic basket with a fairly open weave. This will make it less fiddly to push the stub wires through the weave and secure the flowers in place. Select a basket that has quite high, almost vertical sides.

2 Now take a stub wire and bend it in half. Wrap it around the short stem of a hydrangea head. Leave the two ends of the wire long and poke each through the basket weave at your chosen point. Make sure that one end of the wire goes through the hole above the cane and the other end beneath it. Now secure the head to the basket by twisting the ends of the wire together.

3 Cut off any excess wire and push the twisted section down into the basket where it is out of sight and won't catch on anything.

4 Attach more hydrangea heads using the same method as in step 2. Space the heads evenly around the circumference of the basket. Use an uneven number of hydrangea heads, since odd numbers tend to be easier to design with than even numbers.

5

6

7

8

5 Next, bunch sprigs of sea lavender together and, using stub wires, secure them in position in the same way you did the hydrangea. Arrange them randomly around the basket, not in orderly ranks. Place some vertically and some tilted downward. They don't have to follow the same direction around the basket either – you can arrange them both clockwise and anti-clockwise.

6 Add bunches of scabious in the same manner, building up the thickness of the shape and producing textural interest.

7 Bunch blue larkspur, cutting their long stems short, close to the flower heads. Strip some of the lower blooms off to produce a clean stem. Wire them together and position them around the basket. Fill in any areas that are looking a little empty, completing the circular ring of flowers.

8 With the aid of a glue gun (*see p. 10*), or a strong adhesive, attach red rose heads in groups to conceal the wires binding the bundles together, and also to add a splash of bright colour highlighting throughout the arrangement. All that now remains to be done to finish your basket is to pour in your chosen pot-pourri ingredients. Don't overfill the basket, however – you will need to leave an empty space at the top to create a visual separation between the pot-pourri and dried flowers.

ADVANCED LEVEL

MAKING A TWIG BASKET

Sometimes it is not possible to find a ready-made basket that is perfect for what you have in mind. If this is the case, then you can construct your own.

This twig basket is an excellent example – it takes a little patience, that's all. You can collect the twigs yourself from a nearby woodland, local park or your own garden, something that helps to keep costs to a minimum.

The foundation of the basket is a cut-down fruit tray. A strong cardboard box would also do or, for a smaller arrangement, a shoe box with a few tiny pots would make a pretty display. The concept behind this basket is brought to life only if the flowers are arranged so that they look as if they are actually growing. It is therefore important to choose flowers that look natural in the size of pots you decide to use. Visually, this is an intriguing design – made up of many diverse elements, one on top of the other, to create a feast of colour and texture.

MATERIALS

- Fruit tray
- Hammer and panel pins
- Carpet moss
- Twigs
- Reel wire
- Florist's foam
- Flowerpots
- Bamboo cane
- Glue and glue gun
- Yellow achillea
- Lavender
- Nigella
- Marjoram
- Gerdo rose

1

2

3

1 Obtain a wooden fruit or vegetable tray and cut it down to the size required. By slicing off one end of the tray and repositioning the end wall of the box you can create a tray of any size. Once you have reattached the end piece with the aid of small panel pins, you can start to moss over the wooden container. You may be lucky enough to find a fruit tray small enough for your arrangement without any modification.

2 Take a bundle of twigs and cut them to a length a little longer than the height of the box. Take two long lengths of reel wire. It is easy to join on more lengths of wire throughout the next process, so it is unnecessary to work with wire the same length as the perimeter of the box. Now, bend the reel wire in half and start to bundle up the twigs, securing them in the bend of the wire. Twist the wire together, securing the twigs inside the loop you have made. Do this at both the top and bottom ends of the bundles of twigs. Repeat this step with more bundles and you will start to form a fence-like structure.

3 Once you have constructed a long enough fence using this method, fix the two ends together so that the "wall" fits tightly around the box. This creates the sides of your container. Pack some blocks of florist's foam, cut to size, firmly into the container.

4 Tightly pack more florist's foam shapes into the flowerpots. It doesn't matter how rough this looks since they will not be seen. Ensure that the foam fills the flowerpots all the way down to their bases. Take a length of bamboo cane and pierce the foam through the drainage hole in the bottom of the flowerpots.

Withdraw the cane and spread some glue from the glue gun on to its end. Reinsert the cane into the hole you have already made in the foam and let it set. Leave enough of the cane protruding from the bottom of the pot to secure it in the florist's foam in the basket, using the same method with the glue gun.

5 Fill the basket with more flowerpots, arranging them in a pleasing group. Take some more carpet moss and cover the foam in the pots. Start arranging the dried flowers in the foam, pushing their stems firmly through the thick moss. Leave the yellow achillea stems longer in order to provide some extra height for the arrangement. The lavender is the next to go in. Make sure to angle the stems so that they correspond to the angle of their pot. Next, cut down some nigella and arrange them in their pot.

6 The next flowers to go into their flowerpots are the marjoram and Gerdo roses. All that is left now to be done is to fill in any gaps between the pots with some more carpet moss.

4

5

6

ADVANCED LEVEL

FRONT-FACING ARRANGEMENT

The sophisticated elegance of this front-facing basket will enrich your home and lend warmth and style to any surroundings. Situated in a hallway, it would radiate a welcome to all your visitors. This is a classic design that you will see repeated many times with fresh flowers at weddings, other formal functions and parties.

Usually when florists come to create large, front-facing arrangements using fresh flowers, they will opt to mass the blooms, filling the arrangement with bunched flowers wired into position. This creates a heavy, solid look that is expensive to produce. However, this basket has been especially designed to re-create the look of a fresh-flower arrangement by using dried flowers in exactly the same way as you would freshly cut ones.

The arrangement starts with dried foliage, carefully chosen for its movement and natural look, and then goes on to incorporate dried flowers that have interesting foliage to bring to the design – for example, the red bottle brush and amaranthus. In contrast, the peonies lend a softness of texture to the arrangement. Finally, hydrangea heads have been used in recession, tucked in deep between the other flowers and filling out the arrangement.

1

2

MATERIALS
Prepared basket
Banksia
Eucalyptus spiralus
Nigella orientalis
Red bottle brush
White larkspur
Red amaranthus
Pink-blushed peonies
Ilseta rose
Hydrangea

1 Take a prepared basket (*see pp. 10-17*). This one used here is good and solid, and is heavy enough to provide a secure base for the flower arrangement. Because this is essentially a front-facing design, you will be grouping all the flowers along only one face of the basket. If you use a light, insubstantial basket, you will probably find that the arrangement tends to tip forward all the time unless it is very carefully balanced. If you want to use a light or flimsy basket, you will need to weight it down a little at the back to compensate.

3

4

5

6

2 Start by positioning the dried foliage. Form a fan shape with the banksia. Let the side branches come out horizontally to the basket. Push the long stems deep into the florist's foam so that they are secure and won't drop out when you come to move the arrangement about.

3 Fill in the front section with banksia, cutting the stems shorter so that they don't protrude as much as the two side branches. Again, arrange them so that they fall naturally, going into the foam at right angles. Next, position the eucalyptus spiralus in the same way you did the banksia, filling in the middle of the basket. When viewed from the side, the foliage and flowers should be arranged so that they create a slight curve with the tips of their stems, coming down from the top of the centre stem of banksia to the edge of the bottom foliage.

4 Continue to fill out the shape with nigella orientalis and red bottle brush. Arrange them in the same manner used for the eucalyptus. Keep the stems long to correspond with the other foliage.

5 Next to be arranged are the white larkspur, amaranthus, commonly known as love lies bleeding, and the beautiful peonies. Use these flowers at almost their natural lengths, cutting them down only when you come to the front edge.

6 Scatter red roses throughout the arrangement in small groups of threes and fives. Don't hold the stem too close to the head when pushing it into the foam in case you damage the petals. Take the rose stem from a point near the bottom, holding your hand to form a narrow profile – a little like holding a chopstick – and feed the stem through the mass of flowers into the foam. Once the stem is firmly in place, slowly withdraw your hand. To finish off, use hydrangea heads in deep recession. Gently push them into the arrangement, securing them among the other flowers, which should be dense enough to hold the heads in place (*see opposite*). If you can't achieve this, wire the heads on to canes and push the canes into the foam.

WALL-MOUNTED ARRANGEMENTS

1 Take a prepared twig wreath (*see pp. 10-17*). Then select five bunches of pink larkspur, cutting the stems short, up to about 9in (23cm), and strip away any excess flower heads. Attach the bunches to the wreath using stub wires. Use the same method described for making the pot-pourri basket (*see pp. 26-9*).

2 Using the glue gun, secure the miniature flowerpots to the larkspur. Arrange them in groups so that they cover the stub wires around the flower stems.

3 Carefully cut the pink heli-chrysum heads from their stems and glue just the flowers all around the flowerpots.

4 As the finishing touches, add the flower heads of the pale-blue statice (limonium sinuata) and the eryngium, using the glue gun to attach them securely to the twigs of the wreath.

1

2

3

4

MATERIALS
Prepared wreath
Stub wire
Glue and glue gun
Miniature flowerpots
Pink larkspur
Pink helichrysum
Blue statice
Eryngium

EASY LEVEL

TWIG WREATH

Making wreaths from twigs can be far easier than you would imagine. You need to use supple branches, such as birch or, as used here, Chinese willow (*see also pp. 10-17*).

A wreath such as this can look very eye-catching and most fetching when left in its natural state. However, you can turn it into something really special with the addition of dried flowers, either wired into the weave or glued on to the twigs. Simplicity is the key to this project's success, so keep the design uncluttered and let as much of the branches show through as possible.

This wreath has been decorated with flowers in the pinks and blues of summer. The bright pinks of larkspur and helichrysum against the blue of the eryngium heads and statice encapsulate the essence of a hot summer's day. The flowers have been arranged in five main groupings, each in a different array, to create a random, almost haphazard collection around the wreath. The miniature flowerpots strewn among the flowers help to bring the piece to a visual culmination.

1

2

3

1 If you don't already have a mirror that you can utilize for this project, it is easy to make one out of a piece of rigid backing board and mirror glass cut to a size smaller than the board itself. Attach the mirror to the board with mirror clips. Screw two large-headed screws into the back of the backing board and secure a wire around them to make a hanger. Don't put off this part of the project until the flowers have been arranged or you are bound to cause some damage to your flower arrangement.

2 Now cut strips of florist's foam to size. They should sit around the mirror higher than the surface of the glass. Working with the mirror flat on a tabletop, glue the foam on to the backing board all around the mirror. Use a liberal amount of glue from a glue gun to ensure a firm fixing.

3 Next, mass achillea heads around the mirror, gluing the stems into the foam as you proceed. Start in one place and methodically work your way around the mirror, making sure that you cover all the foam, and especially that there is an even coverage of achillea at the sides. Cut sunflowers down to a short stem, leaving sufficient to secure them into the foam. Again, use the glue gun to reinforce the bond. Place the sunflowers randomly around the frame to give texture and interest to the mirror.

MATERIALS
- Rigid backing board
- Mirrored glass
- Mirror clips
- Screws and screwdriver
- Reel wire
- Glue and glue gun
- Florist's foam
- Achillea
- Sunflowers

EASY LEVEL

ACHILLEA MIRROR

This project demonstrates the endless versatility of dried flowers by moving away from the notion that arrangements need to be confined in some sort of vase or basket. Here, the rich gold of the achillea rivals the opulence of plaster gilt and the sunflowers recall the passion of a Van Gogh painting.

Using the techniques described here, you can bring new life to a tired, old mirror or to one that is perhaps lying unused somewhere because it has an unattractive frame; or you could start from scratch and make a new one altogether. It is easy to attach the florist's foam and you can quickly arrange the achillea to form the body of the frame.

You can use this simple idea as a springboard and then go on to make the other decorated mirrors, such as the hydrangea and rose mirror, shown later in this chapter. As a variation on this basic idea, you could also attempt to create a dried-flower arrangement around a dressing table mirror or surrounding a mirror on a wardrobe or closet door – the variations are endless.

1

2

3

4

EASY LEVEL

WALL VASE

This terracotta replica of a Victorian wall moulding lends itself beautifully to an arrangement of dried flowers. You may be able to find a similar vase in a garden centre, since this one was designed originally as a wall planter. The wheat featuring in this project is symbolic of good fortune and plenty, and it is reminiscent of the times when the harvest meant food-filled days. Tailor your selection of flowers to include a variety of textures and colours. Notice how the protea used in this arrangement contrasts with the wheat, while the lavender echoes its shape and texture.

There are many suitable containers for this project, but ones made of natural materials always seem to work well with dried flowers.

1 Take a block of florist's foam and cut it to a size and shape that will fit inside the the vase. Spread glue on the edges of the foam and slide it firmly into the vase. Hold it tightly for a few moments while the glue sets. Take some gray reindeer moss or lichen moss and cover the foam. There is no need to pin the moss, since the flower stems will secure it in place.

2 Hold up the protea to the prepared container to judge the stem length required. Arrange the heads in a staggered formation.

3 Next, make up bundles of wheat. Cut them down to size and wire them with stub wire. Leave the ends of the wire pointing downward and use them to secure the bunches in the foam. You can also gather the stems in your hand, cut them to size and push them into the foam without wiring them. Now make the horizontal double-ended bunch for the front. This must be wired in place. Use raffia to hide the wire.

4 Arrange the Gerdo roses (*see p. 20*), utilizing the natural foliage of the stems. Place the roses in small groups throughout the wheat and protea, and then take some small bunches of lavender and finish off the arrangement by filling in any empty spaces.

MATERIALS
Terracotta vase
Florist's foam
Glue and glue gun
Reindeer moss or lichen moss
Stub wires
Natural raffia
Protea
Wheat
Gerdo rose
Lavender

1 Take a piece of rigid backing board and mirrored glass cut to a slightly smaller to size. Using large mirror clips, secure the mirror to the board. Screw two large-headed screws into the back of the backing board and secure a wire around the screws to make a firm hanger. Don't wait to do this until after the flowers have already been arranged, since you are then bound to cause some damage to the blooms.

2 Now cut strips of florist's foam to fit right around the outside of the glass. Glue the foam securely to the backing board, making sure that the foam is higher than the glass surface of the mirror and that it is amply thick enough to accommodate the flower stems.

3 Proceed by arranging the hydrangea heads in a massed formation around the mirror to create the frame. Cover all of the foam and ensure that the edges of the frame are also well covered so that no backing board is visible. Look from every angle from time to time to check that coverage is even. Use the glue gun to secure the stems in the foam. When you have covered all of the mirror frame and edges in this fashion, take your roses and position them among the hydrangea heads, pushing and gluing the stems securely into the foam. Arrange them in small groups around the mirror, as you see illustrated in the main picture opposite.

1

2

3

EASY LEVEL

HYDRANGEA MIRROR

The deep, rich, heady notes of this design are reminiscent of the full-blooded qualities of a good Burgundy. These regal tones predominate in the hydrangea, blending into lighter, softer pinks and grayish greens.

The collection of red roses and hydrangeas is a perfect foil for the cool stillness of the mirror. Hydrangea blooms are available from most florists, and when in season they can be bought fresh for home drying. Or if you have a large hydrangea bush in the garden, you could save some of the expense of this project. If you want to do it yourself, pick the hydrangeas just after the blooms have reached their prime, and hang them upside down in a dry, cool, well-ventilated room. To ensure a good circulation of air, avoid bunching too many together.

An alternative method of drying is to place them in a vase so that the air can circulate all around their heads. Leave them in the vase with their stems in just a little water – when the water has evaporated, leave the hydrangeas to dry out completely.

MATERIALS
Rigid backing board
Mirrored glass
Mirror clips
Screws and screwdriver
Reel wire
Glue and glue gun
Florist's foam
Hydrangea heads
Paso Doble rose
Jaguar rose

1

2

3

4

1 Prepare a frame with moss (*see pp. 10-17*). Take strips of sacking or hessian and secure them to the frame with stub wires. Distribute the hessian evenly around the ring in three sections. Make soft folds in the material to give it shape and presence.

2 Concentrate the heads of achillea into five main areas, pushing their strong stems firmly into the moss. Next, take lotus seed heads and wire them as shown here. Take a thick stub wire and push it through the soft sides of the head. Once the wire is halfway through, carefully bend it, bringing both ends of the wire downward at the same time. Keep the legs of the stub wire straight. Hold the lotus head in one hand and, with your other, twist the wire together. Now push the wire through the mossed frame, bringing it out the back of the frame. Pull the wire through from the other side so that the lotus head is pulled into position. Now bend the wires back into the moss and attach them to the frame. Group more of the lotus heads around the wreath using this same technique. Position them at various different angles to show them off to their best advantage.

3 Mass poppy seed heads into the wreath. They have strong stems and so don't need wires. Form them into three principal groups, arranging them closely together, covering the moss in a rough bend that takes them from the outside of the wreath to the inside. This is similar to the way the achillea has been arranged.

4 In between the poppy seed heads you will find just enough room for the odd carthamus head. Fill in with the green buds throughout the wreath in other sections, too. Group the yellow roses close together in any areas that require a little more in terms of a colour highlight. Then, bunch lavender up into little sprigs and wire them together. Bind them with natural raffia to hide the thick stub wires and tie the raffia off in a knot. Wire the lavender into the wreath as you did the lotus heads. Be sure to keep the lavender flat against the wreath, as shown opposite.

INTERMEDIATE LEVEL

COUNTRY WREATH

This rustic wreath with its massed poppy heads and lotus seed heads has a feeling of abundance, due to the layering of flower upon flower. The texture of the hessian sacking adds yet a further dimension and compliments the other natural tones.

The foundation of this arrangement is a mossed wire-wreath frame, easily obtainable from any good florist. You can see how easy it is to make by referring to pages 10-17. It is important to note, however, that once you have made your wreath you must leave it for at least a week to allow the moss right down at the middle to dry out thoroughly. If you don't, the materials used to decorate the wreath will trap the moisture and rot. This applies to any mossed frame or chicken wire shape.

Finding the perfect spot to display your wreath will not be difficult. You might want to hang it on your front door as a sign of hospitality or on the kitchen door at the heart of the household – you could also prop it casually against the display shelf of a dresser.

MATERIALS
Prepared wreath
Sacking or hessian
Stub wire
Achillea
Lotus seed heads
Poppy seed heads
Carthamus
Golden Times rose
Lavender
Natural raffia

1

2

3

4

1 Prepare a block of florist's foam for a wall-mounted arrangement (*see pp. 10-17*). You can work on the spray attached to the wall *in situ*. If this is not possible, lean a board against a convenient surface and fix the block to it with a temporary, but firm, fixing. If you find you can't work using either of these methods, use a tabletop to work on. Occasionally lift the spray up to a wall. This will enable you to correct any errors in overall shape as you proceed. Start your spray off by defining an outline with foliage. Eucalyptus spiralus has been used here. Take two long stems and determine the width of the spray. Next, cut two shorter pieces to size for the top and bottom centre stems. This gives you a grid within which to work. After you have filled in with the rest of the eucalyptus, soften the cross shape by re-aligning the top and bottom stems slightly.

2 Arrange the dock in blocks. The stems should look as though they are radiating out from a central point, splaying out to give an uneven edge to the arrangement. Next, build up the textures using sea lavender, again placed in drifts through the spray. Arrange them closely to the dock to create an obvious association.

3 Now use the hydrangeas deep within the arrangement, making sure that they cover the florist's foam. Push their short stems firmly into the foam.

4 Wire sprigs of lavender together and fill in the shape of the spray to make it full and dense. Leave the stems longer than those of the other flowers to create definition and movement. Next, take two leggy pieces of gnarled branch and push them firmly into the foam. You may find that these pieces are too thick to fit in between the chicken wire. If so, cut strands of wire and open out the shape, giving a larger surface of foam. Place the branches to form a broken diagonal through the spray. Now take five wired lotus seed heads (*see pp. 10-17*). Arrange them in the foam, pushing the wires securely in. Follow the diagonal running through the middle of the spray from top to bottom to create a visual division and provide a focal point.

MATERIALS
Prepared florist's foam
Stub wires
Eucalyptus spiralus
Dock
Lavender
Sea lavender
Gnarled branch or driftwood
Lotus seed heads
Cockscomb (celosia)
Sunflowers
Hydrangeas
White peonies
Pink peonies
Orange carthamus
White Success rose

INTERMEDIATE LEVEL

FREESTYLE SPRAY

This project uses nothing more complicated than a block of florist's foam wrapped in chicken wire and a wire loop to act as a hanger. You can see how to make the basic structure in the chapter on materials and techniques (*see pp. 10-17*).

The materials used here are very textural, and the choice of eucalyptus, lavender, sea lavender and dock is important for their natural recession, as well as adding movement and interest. The muted hues of these flowers are united in the tones of the hydrangeas, and they also blend well with the driftwood and lotus seed heads.

The spray has been arranged in a freestyle fashion, using the flowers in blocks of colour radiating out from the middle to leave an irregular edge. The lotus seed heads and the branches bind the flowers through the middle of the arrangement to give a visual climax.

Throughout the construction of the spray, hold the work up to the wall periodically to make certain that its shape is evolving correctly when it is viewed from all angles.

ADVANCED LEVEL

SWAGGING

This festoon of flowers has its inspiration in the lavish court of Louis XIV. You will find many examples of similar swags decorating the elevations of buildings in masonry relief or glorified in oil paintings.

Garlands of fresh flowers have been used in celebrations in many countries throughout the centuries, re-creating the revelling mood of Bacchanalian feasts. They are still used in this celebratory manner today, typically at weddings where floral swags lend opulence to the proceedings.

Now you can emulate this bountiful effect using dried flowers and stabilized foliage. As your foundation, you will need to build a dry, moss-covered shape made out of chicken wire. Then you can unleash your imagination, creating an exotic and a flamboyant medley of texture and colour. This splendid swagging is obviously at home among ornate furnishings but, equally, the opposite would also be true – a stark, plain background would accentuate its luxurious qualities and make it an irresistible focal point.

MATERIALS
Prepared swag
Prepared twig rings
Natural raffia
Stub wires
Stabilized pittosporum
Stabilized laurel
Cockscomb (celosia)
Sunflowers
Pink peonies
White peonies
Orange carthamus
White Success roses
Glue and glue gun

1 Prepare the moss and chicken wire shape required for your swag (*see pp. 10-17*). This swag is about 35in (90cm) from twig ring to twig ring (*see pp. 40-1*). This swag comprises three separate sections bound together with natural raffia. The middle section of swag is made of one length of chicken wire, 40in (100cm) long, folded around the moss in about half widthways, and then tapered toward the ends and bent to form a sagging shape. The two paddles are about 16in (40cm) long from the ring to the bottom end. They correspond in width with the 6in (15cm) of the thickest point of the swag. You can work up to this point on a tabletop. From here onward, however, you will need to work with the evolving swag hanging on a wall or fixed firmly to a board.

2 Stabilized foliage, such as the pittosporum and laurel in this swag, give the arrangement a fresh and natural feel. Cut sections of the foliage and arrange them in the moss structure. Scatter them randomly throughout the swag. Mass the laurel around the raffia to create a classic look. You can wire the pittosporum and laurel into the moss or, alternatively, use a glue gun to fix the flat leaves of the laurel to the chicken wire.

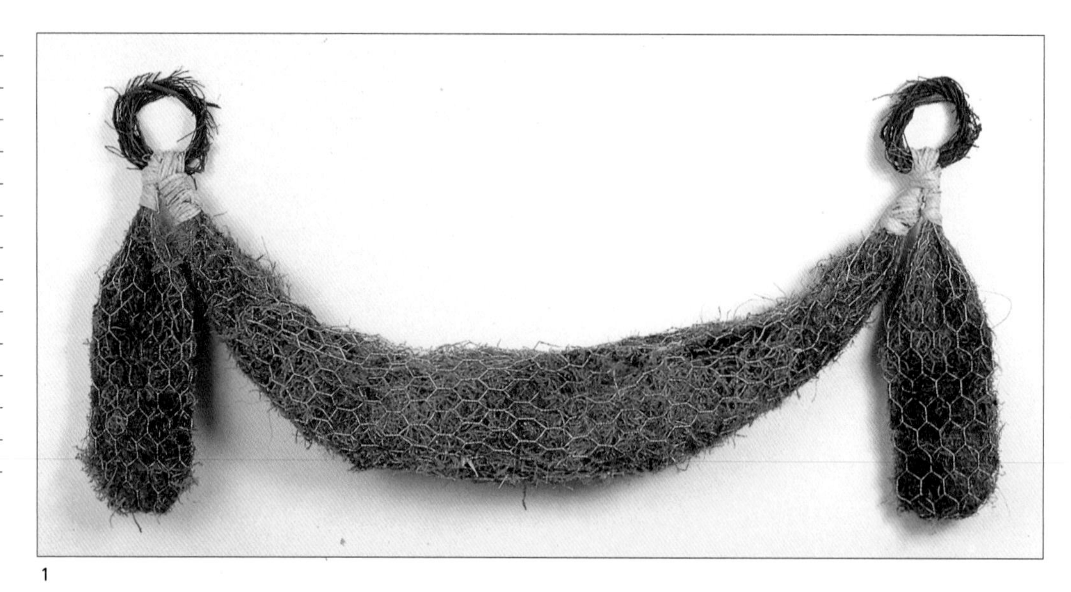

1

2

3

4

5

6

3 Next, push stub wires through the thin, flat sides of some cockscomb heads. Take the largest head and secure it into the foam. Place it slightly off to one side of the centre. Continue to secure more cockscomb heads into the moss. In the example here, five heads have been distributed throughout the swag.

4 Build up the design with sunflowers, pushing their stems straight through into the moss. If the heads are too heavy and start to pull out of the moss, glue them firmly in place. Scatter the sunflowers randomly, some in groups, some congregating around the centre, with the cockscomb creating the focal point of the arrangement.

5 Now take two bunches of dried peonies, one pink and one white. Cut the stems down and group them firmly in the moss. If there are any buds in the peonies, use them in the arrangement protruding slightly above the outline of the swag.

6 Cover the remainder of the moss shape with the heads of orange carthamus. Mass these throughout the swag, ensuring that when it is viewed from every angle the moss is completely covered. This creates a background of the same texture to set off the many colours. Now highlight the swag with groupings of white roses (*see main picture, pp. 52-3*). Gently cradle each rose head in your hand, encircling the flower with your fingers. Blow softly into the middle of the petals to open the head fully. This only works with roses that are on the break.

FREE-STANDING ARRANGEMENTS

EASY LEVEL

TABLE CENTRE

The success of this composition pivots around a suitable candle holder. You could always make one yourself, perhaps one as simple as a piece of wood pierced by a nail to act as candle spike. Once you have found or made your holder, concentrate on the assortment you will be using in the arrangement.

The monochromatic collection brought together here has a natural feel to it: the materials you use, if not actually wood, certainly should have similar properties. Notice how the smoothness of the undulating, contorted willow contrasts with the harshness of the gnarled branch, and the density of the clustered seed heads provides a primary focal point for the piece. The two protea, coupled together, seem to sprout from the wooden shapes to provide a secondary focal point.

Displaying the finished arrangement in the right setting is vital to really bring the piece to life. Echo the qualities of the materials used as much as possible – a scrubbed pine table or a rough, natural wooden surface would be perfect for this project.

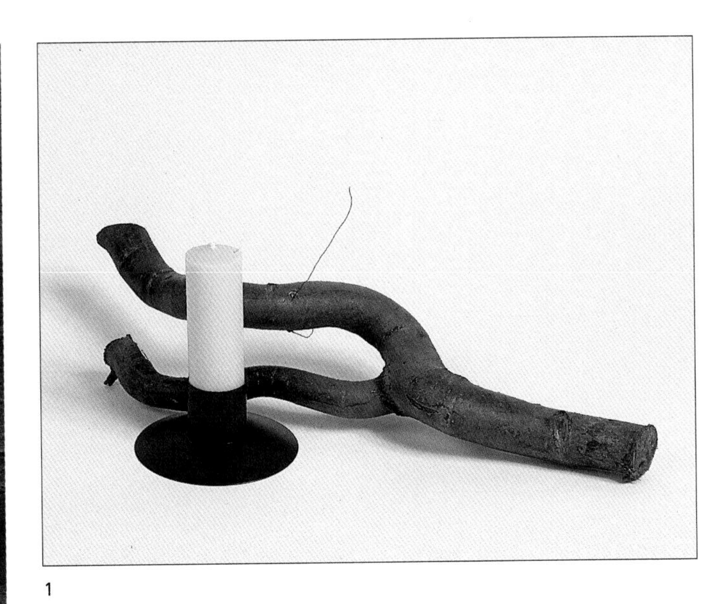

1

1 Take your chosen candle holder. Drill a small hole in the base support section near its outer edge. Now select a contorted willow branch and cut it to size with a saw. Choose a forked branch with an interesting line to it. Drill a small hole in a corresponding section of the branch. Ensure that once the branch is in place, the two holes are close enough together to allow you to pass a wire through and secure branch and candle holder together. The branch should now be held firm, with very little movement possible. If you can't achieve this, use glue to fix the branch to the holder.

2

2 Cross over the willow branch with a piece of gnarled wood. Choose a piece with a bend to cradle the holder. Fix this in place with glue or wire it on to the willow branch. Now glue some lotus seed heads into position. Form them into a strong group, since they will eventually become the focal point of the arrangement.

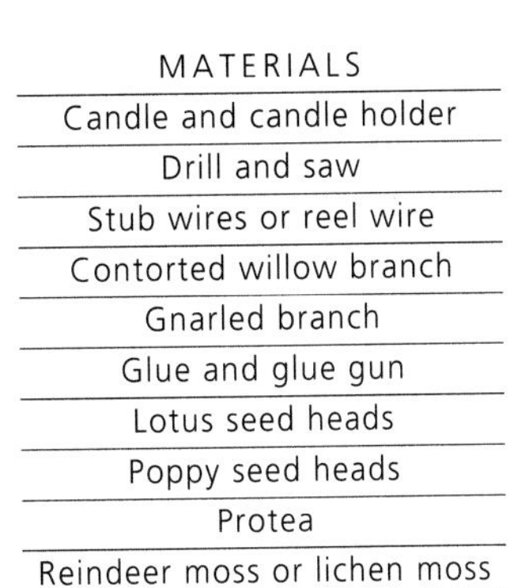

MATERIALS
Candle and candle holder
Drill and saw
Stub wires or reel wire
Contorted willow branch
Gnarled branch
Glue and glue gun
Lotus seed heads
Poppy seed heads
Protea
Reindeer moss or lichen moss

3

3 Build up the formation with more seed heads and any interesting material you feel compliments the piece. Poppy seed heads have been used here, glued in between and around the lotus heads. Use varying sizes of seed head at different levels along the wood. Keep the candle holder itself clear of adornment, however. It would spoil the lines of the arrangement if its base became crammed with different textures. Being able to see the candle holder untouched through the centre of the arrangement creates extra interest. Position the two protea and highlight the grouping comprising the lotus and poppy heads with gray reindeer or lichen moss. Take very small amounts of moss at a time and glue them into the cracks between the seed heads.

1 Take two plastic containers, sized so that one will fit easily inside the other. You can choose between square tubs (as shown here) or cylindrical ones. This concept works equally well with any shape of container.

2 Cover the outside of the larger of the two containers with green reindeer moss. Glue the moss on to the plastic with a glue gun or any strong adhesive. Cover the container all the way up to the top edge, overlapping it slightly. This will ensure that when the fresh flowers are arranged in the inner container none of the base material will be visible.

3 Now, using bright yellow helichrysum, start to decorate the moss. Group the heads around the container in a random fashion, gluing them into position as you did the moss.

4 Place the smaller container inside the outer one. Fill the inner container with water, leaving enough room for the stems of your fresh-flower arrangement without the water overflowing and wetting the dried flowers.

1

2

3

4

MATERIALS

- Two plastic containers – one large, one smaller
- Glue and glue gun
- Green reindeer moss
- Yellow helichrysum heads

EASY LEVEL

CONTAINER FOR FRESH FLOWERS

This container for fresh flowers has been designed with the participation of children very much in mind. With very little preparation or adult supervision, a young child could be involved right from the start in making this attractive and practical container. You may want to use the technique described here yourself as a springboard for your own ideas.

This container consists of two plastic tubs. These need to be of different sizes so that one easily fits inside the other. Make sure there is enough room for you to be able to get your fingers between the two and then to lift the smaller one out at any time.

It is this smaller tub that will eventually become the receptacle for the fresh flowers and water, and you will have to lift and clean it whenever the fresh flowers have gone past their best and have been thrown away. It is important to include this inner tub, otherwise the dried flowers used on the outer one would soon spoil due to the continued handling and cleaning.

1 Plant the amaryllis bulb in a suitable terracotta flowerpot, or any container of your choice. Cover the compost completely with bun moss. Break up some bark into interesting shapes and glue it to the sides of the pot. Position the bark a little higher than the rim of the flowerpot. Then proceed to cover the sides of the pot completely with broken pieces of bark.

2 Bind the bark with lengths of natural raffia. Knot the raffia securely, leaving the ties quite long. When you cut the raffia ends, cut each strand to a different length to give an interesting and varied finish. Now take more bun moss and glue in on to any parts of the terracotta container that are still visible between the pieces of bark. Next, start to build the support structure. Place four lengths of pussy willow deep into the compost. Make sure that the supports are all the same length. If your amaryllis is showing just a small shoot, you will have to use your judgement regarding its mature height and perhaps make adjustments as it grows.

3 Finish off the structure with horizontal struts of willow. Wire them together and bind them with raffia at the joins. Decorate the base with poppy seed heads, attaching them with a glue gun or any strong adhesive.

1

EASY LEVEL

AMARYLLIS BULB HOLDER

An amaryllis in bloom is breathtaking. Before it flowers, however, its allure is less evident. This uninteresting stage in the growth can't be totally disguised, since concealing the growing shoot from sight would mean depriving it of the light it needs to develop. It seems distraction is the answer.

First you need to plant your bulb in a terracotta pot with its growing shoot showing. The decorative moss used here is bun moss. It is important to use a container with adequate drainage to stop the bulb becoming waterlogged. The structure around the amaryllis is intended both to protect and guide the shoot as it grows, but once the plant is heavy with blooms it will also act as a very effective support.

2

3

MATERIALS
Amaryllis bulb
Potting compost
Terracotta flowerpot
Bun boss
Bark
Glue and glue gun
Natural raffia
Reel wire
Pussy willow
Poppy seed heads

INTERMEDIATE LEVEL

MOSSED TREE AND TOPIARY TREE

Many people find it immensely satisfying to emulate the beauty of nature by creating the image and structure of a tree. In the chapter dealing with materials and techniques (*see pp. 10-17*) you will see how to secure a tree "trunk" in a container. Avoid an unnatural look by setting your trunk slightly off the vertical. Don't discount a branch that is bent – it may produce a more natural appearance in the end.

These likenesses of trees have some obvious advantages over the real thing. Seeing that they don't need light or water, you can use them in a dark position that would kill a living plant.

The moss tree is unashamedly a fantasy creation while, at the same time, being quite visually similar to a conventional tree. You can travel farther from nature by using combinations of dried flowers or massing a single type of dried flower, such as rose heads.

The topiary tree is made up of box (buxus) foliage, which you can use freshly cut. Box dries well but it takes on a dull yellow colour. Enjoy its naturalness as long as it lasts, and then why not cheat by restoring its colour with spray paint? Alternatively, you could use a stabilized foliage, although this would be more expensive.

MOSSED TREE

MATERIALS
Prepared trunk and container
Florist's foam ball
Glue and glue gun
Bun moss
Carpet moss
Stub wires

1 Take a prepared tree trunk in a container (*see pp. 10-17*). Push a florist's foam ball on to the top of the trunk. You can buy foam balls ready to use or cut your own from a block of foam. Push the trunk slowly into the foam – this will take quite a bit of pressure. Once it is in place, however, you will find it will easily lift off the trunk. To remedy this, spread glue from a glue gun on top of the trunk and replace the foam ball. Leave it until the foam and wood have securely bonded. Carpet moss has been used here to hide the cement around the trunk and to give the pot a natural finish. Glue the moss into position.

2 Next, take some stub wires and cut them into lengths. Bend the wires to make hairpin shapes and use them to secure pieces of bun moss to the florist's foam ball.

3 Continue to cover the ball with moss using this technique. Slowly build up the shape you require.

4 Ensure that you cover all of the foam, paying particular attention to the area where the trunk enters the foam. Check from all angles that the foam has been completely covered.

1

2

3

4

TOPIARY TREE

MATERIALS
Prepared trunk and container
Florist's foam block
Glue and glue gun
Carpet moss
Box foliage
Spray paint (moss green)

1 Take a prepared trunk in a container (*see pp. 10-17*). Make sure that the trunk is long enough to take the size of the box foliage ball you will be making and still protrude from the bottom. Take a block of florist's foam and cut it in half, creating a rough cube shape. Round off the corners and secure it on top of the trunk. Apply downward pressure until the trunk sinks into the foam. Leave enough foam above the trunk to accommodate the stems of the foliage. Remove the foam, spread glue on top of the trunk, replace the foam and allow the glue to harden. A little carpet moss glued into place has been used to cover the cement.

2 Create a circle with the fresh box, allowing the foliage to radiate out from the foam shape. Keep the box in line to ensure a good circle to work on. This circle divides the foam into two halves.

3 Now repeat this process, this time dividing the foam shape into quarters. Don't worry how rough the outline of the circle is looking, just make sure that it is good and thick.

4 Fill in each quarter of foam with more box. Mass it into the foam, filling the shape out. Keep it in line with the box foliage circles you have already created. You should have a very shaggy looking tree at this stage.

1

2

3

4

5 Cut the rough edges of foliage to form a head with a crisp, round outline. Once you start cutting the foliage, continue around and around the tree, angling your scissors accordingly.

6 Initially, cut your shape to a larger size than you require. Once you have a good outline, trim the foliage back until the head is the right size.

7 The tree is in fact finished at this stage. However, you will find that within about a week or two the fresh green colour of the foliage will start to take on more of a dull yellow look.

8 To restore the foliage's original dark-green colour, hold the tree by its trunk and spray the foliage liberally with a moss-green-coloured spray paint. Hold the tree upside down as well to make sure the paint also reaches the undersides of the leaves.

5

6

7

8

INTERMEDIATE LEVEL

TWIG-CAGED BALL

This construction of sticks and branches, enclosing a massed sphere of vibrant dried flowers has a distinctly architectural feel to it. This is somewhat of a departure from conventional floristry, since the framework is built as opposed to arranged. This creates an entirely new look, one that is innovative and certainly worthy of consideration. Creative florists are continually evolving new forms, some startlingly different in design and style, and hopefully this will challenge many preconceptions about flower arranging

The three structures used in this project are designed to provide a contrast in both size and colour. Each globe is covered in a different material, two of which are enhanced by a special dyeing process to provide an intensely vivid colour that is not normally available in dried flowers. The natural colour of the achillea brings its own richness to the trio, one that is superbly bold and dominant.

MATERIALS

- Florist's foam ball
- Purple botao branco (dyed)
- Yellow achillea
- Red achillea (dyed)
- Long, thick twigs
- Panel pins and hammer
- Thin twigs
- Glue and glue gun

1

2

3

4

1 Take a florist's foam ball – these are available in different sizes and the one you choose depends on the size you want the final construction to be. Choose the dried flower material with which you want to cover the ball. This selection is most important, since the heads of the flower must be small enough to cover the ball evenly while still leaving a distinct ball shape when they are massed closely together. Botao branco has been used here, dyed to a vivid purple colour. As an alternative, you could also use moss to cover the foam ball.

2 Cut the stems to about 1in (2.5cm) and carefully cover the ball with the flower heads. Gently push the stems into the ball until the heads themselves rest on the surface of the foam. Continue to cover the ball until no foam is visible. You may need to arrange a second layer in some places to complete the coverage. If so, push the stems in between the heads already in place. These stems may need to be longer.

3 Measure the height of the foam ball, complete with its massed flower heads. Call this measurement A. Take the long thick twigs, which should all be the same thickness, and cut four of them to this length. Now measure the width of the twigs – they should be roughly the same size. Call this measurement B. Multiply B by two to obtain measurement C. Subtract C from A to give measurement D. Now cut eight twigs to measurement D. These eight twigs will be two widths shorter than the four twigs cut to measurement A. Take two long and two short twigs. Nail a pin half the length of measurement B from each end of one of the long twigs.

5

6

7

Ensure that the panel pins are at right angles to the twig. Centre a short twig end-on to the panel pin and hammer it into place. Repeat this with the other short twig. Nail two more panel pins into the other long twig. Centre up the points of the pins to the two shorter lengths attached to the other twig, and hammer them securely in.

4 Hammer pins into the four corners of the square. Position one of the short twigs on the point of one pin and hammer the other end into place. Repeat at each corner.

5 Place the prepared ball into the cage structure, taking care not to disturb the flower heads.

6 Make the top of the structure as you did the base. Secure the twig square with panel pins, enclosing the ball.

7 Cut lengths of thin twigs to size and glue them to the cage, taking a diagonal line from corner to corner. Repeat this to form an X shape on each side of the cage construction.

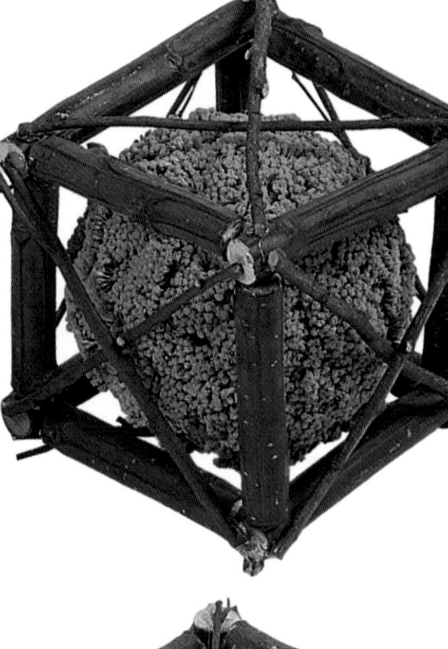

Make other structures and flower balls in varying sizes and colours. Achillea has been used for the balls here. The naturally yellow achillea heads have been cut down into small portions. The red achillea has been dyed to give it a dazzling colour. These small heads are ideal for covering the foam without marring the ball's underlying shape.

INTERMEDIATE LEVEL

ACHILLEA CONSTRUCTION

The inspiration for this project comes from one of the stages of basket weaving. Taking this one step further, by involving the concept of a tied bunch of flowers, it evolves into the highly stylized construction seen opposite.

The achillea used here has been selected for its uniformity. The stems have been stripped of foliage so that they resemble strands of wicker. Soaking the stems in hot water makes them pliable and easy to bend – particularly important when arranging the configuration at the top of the design.

The box containing the display is made of ridged cardboard, cut to an appropriate size and glued together. The watermarked black moiré helps to provide an oriental flavour.

1 Prepare a square container with foam and moss (*see pp. 10-17*). This container has been made out of thick cardboard. Cut squares out of the cardboard and glue them edge to edge to make an open box. Cover the container with black moiré. Take nine stems of achillea, selecting them for the quality and uniformity of their heads. Cut them to the same size. Strip off the foliage and take about ¾in (2cm) off one stem and secure it in the centre of the foam. It must be firmly in place so it is best to glue it into position.

2 Take the remaining achillea and soak the stems in a bowl of hot water. Position one stem at a corner of the box and take the head up to meet the central flower. Because the middle stem is shorter, the outer stem must bend to meet it. Secure it in place with reel wire. The head should now be facing the diagonal corner opposite the base of the stem. Position the next stem halfway between the two corners. Bring it underneath the other two heads and position it facing the opposite side of the box.

3 Continue in this fashion, working right around the sides of the box. Weave each achillea head into place, wrapping the reel wire around the stems to bind them. Now take a strip of black moiré and tie it around the stems, making sure to hide the reel wire.

1

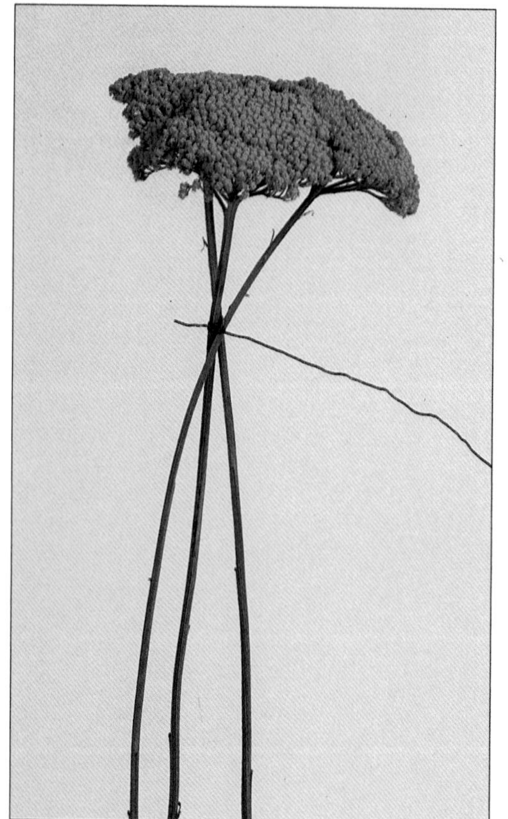

2

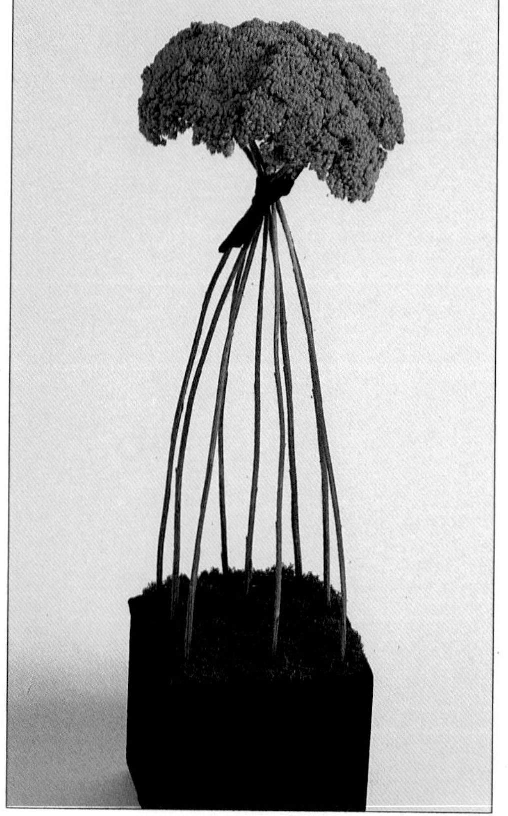

3

MATERIALS
Prepared container covered in black fabric
Florist's foam
Green reindeer moss
Achillea
Reel wire
Glue and glue gun

ADVANCED LEVEL

WHEAT AND ALCHEMILLA

This design encapsulates the very essence of the countryside, with its golden fields of wheat edged with wild flowers. And here the effect has been wonderfully offset by the choice of a handsomely weathered flowerpot to contain the whole arrangement.

This project brings together two contrasting styles. Notice the meticulous manner with which the wheat has been arranged to give the impression of control and uniformity, while the roses, poppy seed heads and alchemilla (commonly known as ladies' mantle) have a rambling, informal quality.

The design is divided into three equally important parts – the wheat, the flowers and, finally, the pot itself. This flowerpot isn't just the container for the arrangement, it is also an integral part of the concept. It echoes the outline of the sheaf head – narrow at the bottom and splaying out toward the top. The flowerpot also reiterates the cool restraint of the wheat, rounding off the composition to perfection. As a container, it also lends the important ingredient of height, giving the arrangement elegant dimensions and a subtle sophistication.

You could, in fact, finish the arrangement by step 5 (*see overleaf*) if you wished. By that stage the structure is almost an arrangement in itself. If you do finish there, conceal the stub wires with some form of binding, such as natural raffia or sacking.

MATERIALS
Flowerpot
Florist's foam
Glue and glue gun
Stub wires
Natural gray reindeer moss or lichen moss
Wheat
Alchemilla mollis (ladies'mantle)
Poppy seed heads
Gerdo rose

1 Take a suitable flowerpot, quite large in size, and about 10in (25cm) high. Fill the pot with florist's foam, leaving a level top. Now take two full blocks of foam and secure them together with hot glue and stub wires bent into large hairpin shapes. Fasten them on to the flat surface of the florist's foam in the container. Cover with lichen moss or gray reindeer moss.

2 Divide the wheat into equal bunches – about 16 in all. Cut them down to suitable lengths and either wire them together or just hold them in your hand and push them securely into the foam around the edge of the blocks.

3 Keeping the tops of the ears of wheat level with each other, fill in the rest of the foam. Arrange them in rows of four along the top of the foam.

4 Now measure the distance between the top of the wheat to the base of the foam blocks. Cut lengths of wheat to this length, again keeping the ears level. Wire them into thin bunches. Next, place them up against the sides of the foam and pin them securely into place with the stub wires. The bottoms of the stems don't penetrate the foam in the container itself; they are only supported by the wires.

1

2

3

4

5

6

7

8

5 Continue to surround the foam with bunches of wheat until it is completely covered and no foam can be seen when viewed from any angle. In some places you may have to add a second layer of wheat in order to achieve complete coverage.

6 Next, start to mass the alchemilla mollis around the wheat. Push the graceful stems firmly into the florist's foam in the container. Arrange the stems as though they are growing naturally out of the pot, angling them to give a sense of movement and fluidity. As you move around the wheat, make sure that the alchemilla is higher than the line of stub wires.

7 Now arrange some of the poppy seed heads in a random fashion, as if they, too, were growing naturally. Use different heights and sizes of poppies. Push some heads deep into the alchemilla mollis near the stems of wheat. Continue to do this right around the arrangement.

8 To finish off, you need to incorporate the peach-coloured Gerdo roses – but use restraint here. Arrange the roses through the alchemilla mollis in much the same way you did the poppy seed heads in step 7 – in a random and natural fashion.

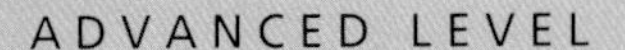

FLOWERPOT MAN

Children and adults alike will have tremendous fun making this flowerpot figure. You will readily find suitable terracotta flowerpots of all sizes at garden centres and hardware stores. The smallest terracotta pots are ideal for creating the hands and feet.

When you choose the flowerpots for your figure, set them up roughly in a body shape, using the picture here as a guide. Keep the terracotta pots spaced out in a proper relationship to the different parts of the body they are representing, and also try to keep all the body parts in realistic proportions, no matter how small your figure is.

A child will need some supervision while making this project. An adult will, for example, have to make the holes in the sides of the flowerpots with an electric drill. You should also take some basic precautions when using long lengths of reel wire. Using lengths suitable to connect all the pots can be hazardous. The wire has a tendency to curl up at the cut end and take on a life of its own, so wear some form of eye protection.

1

2

3

4

MATERIALS
28 flowerpots
Reel wire
Drill
Twigs
Florist's foam
Bamboo cane
Glue and glue gun
Natural raffia
Stub wires
Sphagnum moss
Scissors
Eye goggles

1 Take the terracotta flowerpot you have selected to be the lower part of the torso and drill a small hole in each side, approximately where the hip joint will be. Drill a hole in one of the pots selected for the legs. Thread a length of reel wire through these holes. Double the wire into two thicknesses to provide extra strength. Now wrap the wire at a suitable point around a twig just to hold the wire in place.

2 The wire should be long enough to go through all of the flowerpots you have selected for the legs and the lower torso. Take some dry sphagnum moss and half fill the small flowerpot. Stuff it firmly in.

3 Thread another of the leg flowerpots along the wire and then half fill it with sphagnum moss as well.

4 Repeat this with a third flowerpot and pull them all together so they make one continuous piece. Now thread on another flowerpot, this time the other way around. Cup the two flowerpots together facing each other to form the knee joint. Fill the new flowerpot with moss and a little more between the two facing pots to make a knee cap. Place a second flowerpot up to the other one, facing the same direction. Half fill this flowerpot with moss.

5 Take a small flowerpot you have selected to become a foot. Face it end-on to the previous pot and thread the remainder of the reel wire through. Take another twig. Wrap the end of the reel wire around the twig and roll it down until it is flush with the bottom of the pot.

5

6

7

8

6 Fill this foot with sphagnum moss. Now repeat the process of building up the flowerpots to create the second leg. Pull the reel wire tight when fixing the first flowerpot with the twig at the hip, securing both legs into place. Follow the steps through again until the flowerpot man has two complete legs. Wedge some florist's foam, cut to size, in place to accommodate a bamboo cane "spine". Alternatively, you could fill the flowerpot with quick-drying cement for a really secure fixing. This, however, will make your flowerpot man very heavy.

7 Once this is done, start work on the top half of the torso, preparing the arms using exactly the same technique you employed for the legs. Follow the stages all the way through to step 6, stopping once you have filled the hands with moss. Now carefully spread a little hot glue along the rim of the lower torso flowerpot. Thread the bamboo cane through the small drainage hole at the top of the upturned flowerpot. Gently lower the flowerpot down until it joins, rim to rim, the bottom half of the torso. Quickly wipe away any excess glue with a damp cloth. Slip the flowerpot you have selected for the neck over the bamboo cane. Using the glue gun, fix this pot into position. If your flowerpot is so small that the hole in the top is not large enough for the bamboo cane, use a closed pair of scissors to widen the hole a little by gently wearing away the edges of the terracotta.

8 Take the last flowerpot, the one you have selected to be the head, and fill it with florist's foam, leaving about a ¼in (1cm) gap at the top. To form the flowerpot man's hair, first wire one end of a length of natural raffia into the pot and cut it to length. Rewire the new end of raffia and continue in this way until the flowerpot is full. Take a pair of scissors and trim and shape the raffia to give your flowerpot man a hair cut. You could make a flowerpot woman with long braids or pigtails. (Dried flowers could also be used in place of raffia.) Finally, secure the head to the bamboo cane and glue it into position.

SPECIAL OCCASIONS

1 Take a prepared basket in the shape of a heart (*see pp. 10-17*). This basket has been pulled into a better shape with reel wire. Cut the florist's foam to the shape of the basket and gently push it on to the reel wire. This will leave an indentation showing where you have to cut the cross. It would be wasteful to cover the foam with moss, since the rose heads will be so close together you should not be able to see any of the foam between them.

2 Take some red Mercedes roses and cut down the stems. Push the shortened stems of the roses into the foam and form the outline of the heart with the flower heads arranged very close together.

3 Fill in the middle of the heart with more rose heads. Make sure that you keep them all level with each other.

4 Once the basket is full with roses, tuck some reindeer or lichen moss under the heads of the outer roses. You can glue the moss securely into position if necessary with a glue gun.

1

2

3

4

MATERIALS
Basket
Reel wire
Glue and glue gun
Florist's foam
Mercedes rose
Natural reindeer moss or lichen moss

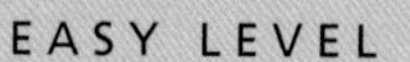
EASY LEVEL

VALENTINE BASKET

As St Valentine's Day becomes increasingly popular, it gets harder and harder to find fresh gift ideas to exchange as love tokens on 14 February. But what could be more romantic than to give somebody your very own heart?

This project is simple to construct and, once you have obtained all the materials required, it is also quick to make. The basket itself was no trouble to find, but its shape needed defining a little. This was done with reel wire, threaded through the weave of the basket and attached at the opposite side. The edges were then pulled closer together at certain points to create a much stronger heart-shaped outline.

Massed flower heads have been incorporated into many of the designs featured in this book. And here it is the Mercedes rose that brings the heart-shaped basket to life with colour.

You could give this basket as a present to your Valentine, or you could just as easily use it as a table centre for an intimate, candle-lit dinner on this most romantic of all days.

EASY LEVEL

CHRISTMAS GIFT WRAP

Receiving presents at Christmas is always a thrill, no matter how old you are. When you give a carefully chosen gift, the amount of thought that has gone into it is always evident. Now you can take this a stage further by creating a unique gift wrap as well.

This gift has been wrapped in a traditional style. The starting point is the dark-green handmade paper. You can then proceed to adorn the parcel with a feast of colours and textures. The tartan ribbon, shot through with strands of gold, has also been tied off in a beautiful bow. Fresh pine and pine cones are easy to come by and here they have been glued to the paper as additional decoration, but make sure that the paper you choose is thick enough to absorb the adhesive safely. Finish off with dried red roses and gold-sprayed poppy seed heads.

You can adapt this idea to Christmas decorations, for use year after year. Try making very small boxes to hang on your tree, or incorporate them in festive swagging and table arrangements.

1

2

3

4

MATERIALS
Green handmade paper
Green, red and gold tartan ribbon
Glue and glue gun
Blue pine
Pine cones
Mercedes roses
Poppy seed heads
Gold spray paint

1 Take your present and wrap it in thick paper. The paper used here is a dark-green handmade paper, but many good-quality machine-made papers would also be perfectly suitable, as long as they are thick enough to absorb the adhesive without it seeping through to the present beneath. Tie a ribbon around the gift, crossing the length underneath the parcel and fastening it at the top.

2 Take a prepared bow (*see pp. 10-17*) and place it in the middle of the two ties, and secure the bow to the parcel.

3 With a glue gun, fix some of the sprigs of blue pine to the paper. The paper must be thick enough to absorb the hot glue without harming the present beneath. If you are in any doubt about this, use a layer of thick tissue paper first, wrapped right around the present, to protect it from harm. Position the twigs of blue pine in a rough diagonal, from corner to corner.

4 With the glue gun, fix the pine cones on to the package. Dot the cones randomly through the diagonal. Next, remove the stems from the Mercedes roses and glue the heads on to the pine. Finally, take some of the small poppy seed heads, spray them with the gold paint, wait until they are dry and then glue them on to the arrangement where they will create the most impact.

1

2

3

4

1 Take a florist's foam ball and a block of foam. Judge the size the head should be in proportion to the foam ball body. Cut the block to size, forming the foam into a round shape with flat sides. Put the foam ball to one side. Cover the head shape with the achillea flowers cut down into small segments.

2 Once you have completely covered the foam shape, take two large berries for the eyes and glue them into place with the glue gun. Now take an appropriate-sized poppy seed head and cut off the flat end. Cut down each side to the base of the seed head. Cut the stem down to size and position it securely in the florist's foam to act as the beak.

3 Prepare the florist's foam ball for the chick's body in the same way as the head. Take a prepared basket with a covering of natural reindeer moss (*see pp. 10-17*). Take two stems of achillea and strip away the foliage. Secure one stem into the foam ball at an angle. Push in the second stem a little farther back. Bend this stem to form the backward knee joint of the chick. Secure them both into the foam of the basket. Next, position a small spike of achillea stem to act as the neck.

4 Make three toes for each foot with achillea stems and glue them to the moss, in the correct position in relation to the legs. Glue the end on to the leg close to the moss. Now shape some achillea heads into wings and a tail by cutting off excess flowers. Arrange them on the achillea-covered ball of the chick's body. The last section to be fitted is the head to complete the Easter chick.

EASY LEVEL

EASTER CHICK

This Easter chick is great fun to make and it is an ideal project for both children and adults. It is not at all complicated and won't take long to construct. To create the head and body of the chick, use the method for making the flower ball shown on pages 70-3.

The achillea have been cut back to the point where the flower heads can be dismantled, and only small portions of them are used at a time to give a close covering for the foam shapes. Notice in the main picture above that massing the portions of the achillea flowers in this fashion produces an effect similar to that of the fluffy down of a chick. Be sure to leave enough stem on the poppy head that will become the chick's beak, however, to secure it into the florist's foam.

Once you have finished your model you can easily dismantle it and hide it away before quickly reassembling it on Easter morning. Imagine the surprise on everybody's face to wake up and discover this amusing little chick, perhaps with a basket brimming over with delicious chocolate Easter eggs.

MATERIALS
Prepared basket
Florist's foam
Florist's foam ball
Glue and glue gun
Reindeer moss
Achillea
Two large berries
One poppy seed head

1

2

3

EASY LEVEL

CHRISTMAS TWIG WREATH

Traditional Christmas decorations may not suit the style of your home, and so this elegant Christmas twig wreath is an alternative to the pine wreath shown on page 102-3.

The stylized feel to this wreath is increased by the gilding of the dried materials. Notice that only the undersides of the cones have been sprayed with paint, and just the top surfaces of the lotus seed heads. This leaves some natural colour to act as a contrast.

The other flowers, such as the exotic protea and the poppy seed heads, have been held at a distance from the spray can and only lightly sprayed to create a softly mottled, metallic effect.

Overall, the altered image of the birch twigs gives a more modern flavour to the wreath. The green paint gives a matt finish to the branches, one that sets off the shine of the golden objects around the circumference.

MATERIALS
Birch twigs
Stub wires
Reel wire
Green spray paint
Gold spray paint
Glue and glue gun
Protea
Lotus seed heads
Poppy seed heads (both large and small)
Pine cones

1 Spray birch twigs with green paint, let them dry, and form them into a wreath (*see pp. 10-17*). Spray the wreath again to repair any damaged paint. Take some protea heads and lightly spray them at arm's length with gold-coloured paint. When dry, glue them to the twig wreath.

2 Spray the tops of some lotus seed heads with gold paint. Allow them to dry. Take stub wires and pierce right the way through. Bend the wire down, twist and wire the heads to the wreath.

3 Spray the undersides of the pine cones with gold paint. To do this, take a wired pine cone, turn it upside down with its base facing you, and spray the cone in one direction. The paint will reach the outside edge only, leaving the inner part its natural colour. This works only on open cones. Attach the pine cones to the wreath, grouping them around the other components. Next, lightly spray large and small poppy seed heads with gold paint, allow them to dry and attach them to the wreath.

EASY LEVEL

MOTHER'S DAY POSY

Giving fresh flowers as a present on Mother's Day is always a thoughtful gesture, but it is only a short time before they wilt and die and have to be thrown away. You could, however, give this beautiful arrangement of dried flowers, which will last and last.

The traditional country garden feel of this posy comes from the informal use of the flowers. The bright yellow of the roses echoes the golden tones of the achillea, and the boldness of the dark-blue larkspur contrasts with the frothy textures of the foliage. Anybody would be appreciative of such a posy.

A small posy like this would be just as well received as a formal florist's bouquet. And with some clever cutting, once the posy is completed you can achieve a standing arrangement of flowers that doesn't need a container.

1

2

MATERIALS
Yellow Golden Times rose
Yellow achillea
Blue larkspur
Hypericum
Linseed
Natural raffia

3

1 First, carefully prepare your flowers. Take the roses and remove all the thorns. Separate the rest of the flowers so that they are easy to grasp and pick up using only one hand. Now take a selection of flowers made up from all the different ones you have chosen and prepared, and form them into a small, attractively shaped bunch.

2 Hold the bunch in your least-used hand (for example, your left hand if you are a right-hander). This will leave your other hand free to arrange the flowers. Form more little collections of your flower selections and gather them in your hand. Weave the flowers so that they spiral out from the principal central bunch.

3 Repeat this process until you have used up all the flowers and your bunch has taken on a good, round shape. Secure the stems with natural raffia tied in an attractive bow. Cut off the hanging raffia ties. Then carefully cut the stems of the flowers, leaving them flat enough for the bunch to stand up on its own. Cut the stems slightly shorter at the centre and you will find that the outside stems tend to splay out to provide additional support for your posy.

EASY LEVEL

BIRTHDAY GIFT IDEAS

Coming up with original birthday gift ideas can be difficult, so why not give an arrangement of dried flowers that you have made? The personal nature of the gift is sure to be appreciated.

Pot-pourri can be used in many ways, adding the wonderful dimension of fragrance to your gift. The sacking, decorated with a tiny bunch of flowers, has been filled with pot-pourri for a drawer or wardrobe or closet.

The round box also contains pot-pourri. After shaking the mixture, remove its lid to release the fragrance. Another box, made of bark, has been filled with delicious chocolates and decorated with yellow helichrysum.

Pomanders can be made from fruits covered with cloves or you could use a foam ball. Decorated with miniature rose heads, it makes a handsome gift, while the roses adorning the hair band make it a very special present for a young girl to wear on her birthday.

The decorated picture frame is a delight, and the lavender surrounding the photograph makes it a present of great sentimental value. Or why not try another simple idea – bound roses in a sack? The bright-red blooms massed together make a startling contrast to the rough hessian.

The miniature basket filled with flowerpots and flowers is a variation on a larger basket earlier in the book (*see pp. 30-3*), and the concept works just as well when scaled down.

PHOTOGRAPH FRAME

MATERIALS
Picture frame
Lavender
Glue and glue gun

Take any suitable picture frame. The one used here is made from recycled paper. Select stems of lavender and carefully glue them in strips right around the frame with hot glue from a glue gun. Use the glue very sparingly on the lavender stems. Gently press each down on to the paper frame and hold it firmly until the glue has set and bonded. Repeat this process until you have covered the entire face of the frame.

POMANDER

MATERIALS
Florist's foam ball
Natural raffia
Stub wire
Doris Rijkes roses

Take a florist's foam ball and attach some natural raffia securely to it using a stub wire. Wrap the raffia right around the foam ball, dividing the foam into quarters. Tie it off at the top and then plait the strands of raffia together. Fill in the four sections of the foam with densely packed rose heads. A variety of spray rose has been used for this mini project.

POT-POURRI BAG

MATERIALS
Hessian sacking material
Needle and thread
Pot-pourri ingredients
Lavender
Achillea
Orange carthamus
Stub wire
Natural raffia

Take a strip of hessian material and sew it into a pouch-shaped container. Fill your container with your favourite mixture of pot-pourri ingredients. Using a small selection of dried flowers, such as lavender, achillea and orange carthamus, make up a small posy. Wire it together with a stub wire and then bind the stems with natural raffia. Now secure the posy on to the pot-pourri bag with more raffia and finish it off with a small bow.

POT-POURRI BOX

MATERIALS
Round wooden box
Natural raffia
Glue and glue gun
Natural reindeer moss or lichen moss
Poppy seed heads
Pot-pourri ingredients

Select a suitable round wooden box (this one formerly contained chocolate-covered coffee beans) complete with lid. Wrap natural raffia around the sides of the box and glue it into position with a glue gun. Tie the raffia off into knots. Repeat this procedure with the sides of the lid. Now cover the top of the lid with reindeer or lichen moss and glue it into place. Arrange regular-sized poppy seed heads on the moss, taking care to keep all the heads level. Glue them down. Finally, fill the box with sweet-smelling pot-pourri.

ROSES IN A SACK

MATERIALS
Hessian sacking container
Florist's foam
Natural reindeer moss or lichen moss
Mercedes roses
String

Take a suitable container, such as this stiffened hessian sack, and fill it with florist's foam. If you can't find a ready made sack, then sew your own from a strip of suitable material. Place a little natural reindeer or lichen moss on top to cover the foam. Cut all the Mercedes rose stems to the same length and arrange them in the foam. Ensure that the heads are all level. Bind the sack and the roses with lengths of string and tie them off with a knot.

MINIATURE FLOWERPOT BASKET

MATERIALS
Small basket
Florist's foam
Carpet moss
Glue and glue gun
Terracotta flowerpots
Lavender
Yellow achillea
Achillea ptarmica (sneezewort)

Take a miniature basket with a handle and fill it with florist's foam. Next, take three miniature flowerpots and fill them with foam also. Cover the florist's foam in the terracotta flowerpots with a little carpet moss. Arrange the flowerpots in the basket so that they are at interesting angles and press them firmly down into the foam, leaving indentations. Now glue them securely into position with hot glue from a glue gun. Next, take the flowers, which you have specifically selected for their small heads. Here, achillea heads have been cut down in their component sections. Arrange the heads in the flowerpots so that they look like they are growing naturally. Fill in any gaps around the flowerpots with some more of the carpet moss to hide the foam.

CHOCOLATE BOX

MATERIALS
Square bark container
Yellow helichrysum
Glue and glue gun
Chocolates

Obtain a suitable square container – the one used for this birthday gift idea is a basket made of bark with handles. Glue yellow helichrysum flower heads on to the edge of the basket. Select the helichrysum heads for their regular size, but a few small heads will be extremely useful for adding decoration under the basket's handles. Using hot glue from a glue gun, secure the heads to the rim of the basket. Hold each flower head in place until the glue has set. Now fill the basket with chocolates of your choice.

HAIR BAND

MATERIALS
Plastic hair band
Natural raffia
Glue and glue gun
White Success roses

Select a suitable plastic hair band and bind it with natural raffia, gluing it into position with a glue gun. Cover the plastic hair band completely. Next, using the glue gun, stick rose heads on to the top surface of the hair band. Arrange the largest heads in the middle of the band and taper down to the smaller buds toward either end of the band. Make sure to leave enough room for the band to slip behind the ears without the roses getting in the way.

1 Take a prepared heart-shaped wreath made of moss and chicken wire (*see pp. 10-17*). Once you have prepared your moss and chicken wire, it is an easy job simply to bend it carefully into a heart shape. Remember to let the wreath stand for at least a week (depending on conditions), until the moss has completely dried out, before you start to work on it.

2 Wire small sprigs of sea lavender together with thick stub wires. Push the wires firmly into the moss structure. Starting at the top of the heart, work downward to the point, arranging the flowers so that they always travel in the same direction down this side. Once you have reached the point, start at the top of the other half of the heart. The sea lavender should now travel in the opposite direction, meeting at the point. Now fill in the top section, accentuating the dip in the middle.

3 Cut strong stub wires into lengths and bend them into hair pin shapes. Take small handfuls of green reindeer moss and pin them into place along the edges of the wreath. Continue doing this until you have built up a solid wall of moss all the way around the outside, totally covering the underlying moss and chicken wire structure. Repeat this with the inside of the wreath.

4 Group the rose heads together, setting them into the sea lavender. The Paso Doble roses and the Jaguar roses have been used for this project. Using a glue gun, stick the rose heads securely into position.

1

2

3

4

MATERIALS
Prepared wreath in chicken wire and moss
Stub wires
Glue and glue gun
Sea lavender
Green reindeer moss
Paso Doble rose
Jaguar rose

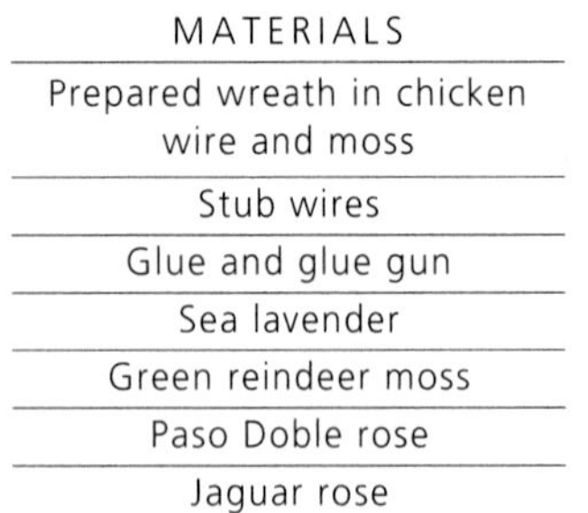

INTERMEDIATE LEVEL

VALENTINE WREATH

It is from the Victorian era that our celebrations of St Valentine originate. A popular idea then was sending cards made from paper and lace that opened out into pop-up tableaux portraying scenes of profound love. Inspired by their observance of St Valentine's Day, and combined with the Victorians' love of dried flowers, this heart-shaped wreath has been created.

The underlying wreath is made from chicken wire, which is then formed into a heart shape. The sea lavender's delicate quality is reminiscent of the lace used in those early Victorian cards, and it becomes the ideal background for the roses. The red rose is always synonymous with love and it has become a symbol of St Valentine. The roses used here are the two-tone Paso Doble and the deep-red Jaguar.

1

2

3

4

MATERIALS
Prepared chicken wire wreath with moss
Blue pine
Reel wire
Stub wires
Glue and glue gun
Pine cones
Walnuts
Exotic dried fruit slices
Cinnamon sticks
Jacaranda roses
Gold-coloured paper ribbon

INTERMEDIATE LEVEL

CHRISTMAS PINE WREATH

A stunning door wreath to welcome in the spirit of Christmas can be one of the strongest images of this festive occasion. Filled with all the ingredients of the celebration, this fresh pine ring is a sure sign of your hospitality during the party season.

A distinct advantage in using the blue pine is that it will keep its needles throughout the Christmas period. If, however, holly is incorporated, it may dry out quite quickly and need to be replaced before the New Year.

The wreath frame used for this project has four integral candle holders designed for dual use. These allow you to use the wreath either as an advent wreath, placed flat on a table, for example, or it can be hung by a wire, secured on a nail or door knocker.

The natural collection used to adorn the ring has close connections with traditional Christmas. Sliced dried pineapple and exotic fruits jostle for attention among the pine cones, walnuts and bundles of cinnamon sticks topped off with dried rose heads.

1 Take a prepared wreath frame (*see pp. 10-17*). Using reel wire, bind sprigs of blue pine into position. Continue around the wreath, working the blue pine in the same direction, until the frame is covered and the pine has created a full base on which to work.

2 Wire the bases of some pine cones and secure them to the wreath by pushing strong stub wires through the moss and out the other side. Now bend the wire back into the moss so that it holds the pine cone firmly in place.

3 Take some walnuts and prepare them with wires. Hold the nut with the bottom part facing you. Gently poke the blade of a scissors between the join of the nut's shell. Stop just before the nut starts to crack. Withdraw the blade and replace it with a stub wire bent in half. Use the legs of the stub wire to secure the nut to the wreath. Make hairpin shapes out of stub wires and pierce dried pineapple slices. Once you have prepared enough, start to decorate the wreath. Secure them in the same way as the pine cones.

4 Glue more dried fruit slices to the surfaces of the pineapple. Next, make a bow with paper ribbon and cut the ties at the end into V shapes. Secure the bow to the wreath with a stub wire. Cut three sticks of cinnamon to the same size, wrap a thick stub wire around them and firmly fix them together by twisting the stub wire legs together. Glue a rose head to the cinnamon sticks, making sure to hide the stub wire. Make some more of these bundles and arrange them on the wreath.

INTERMEDIATE LEVEL

PINE CONE CHRISTMAS TREE

This unusual idea for Christmas can be used in a variety of settings. For example, you could use it as a table centre – unlike the usual floral arrangements that take up so much of the table, this design has a narrow base and leaves plenty of room for dishes.

The wine-red velvet that covers the container of this pine cone Christmas tree contrasts strongly with the dark tartan ribbon used to secure the material around the trunks. The velvet links to the roses, helping to accentuate their colour, while the mass of pine cones creates a textural background.

Although it is made of long-lasting materials, you could always revamp it if it suffers any damage or just change the ribbons to create a different colour theme from time to time.

You will find details of how to secure the tree trunk in the container in the chapter dealing with materials and techniques (*see pp. 10-17*). Although this design uses more than one trunk, the same fixing method applies.

1 Take a prepared trunk in a container (*see pp. 10-17*). This design actually has three trunks for added interest, but the fixing technique remains the same. Secure some blocks of florist's foam on to the top of the trunk. Using a glue gun, glue the foam into position for extra strength.

2 Next, wrap a skin of chicken wire around the foam. Cover the florist's foam and the chicken wire skin with moss, wired into position. The moss will eventually be covered and you will be able to see only small amounts through the gaps in between the pine cones. A dark-purple reindeer moss has been used in this project.

3 Once the moss has been wired to the foam with stub wires, and it completely covers the shape, start to fix stub wires to your pine cones (*see p. 11*). Mass the pine cones in groups that almost cover the moss, leaving just small areas free for other decoration. If you would like to place more decorations on the tree but have no space, just remove some of the cones and replace them with your chosen material. Arrange Jacaranda rose heads in the gaps left between the pine cones. Group some of the rose heads together in twos and threes around the tree. The stems of the roses will go into the florist's foam easily so there is no need to wire them into the arrangement. Next, take a length of burgundy-coloured velvet and wrap it around the container and secure it to the trunk with the end of a stub wire. Now, cover the wire fixing with a tie of tartan ribbon. Make a bow and fix it into position using the ribbon ties, and then cut them to an appropriate size.

4 Next, wire walnuts to the tree using thick stub wires (*see step 3, p. 103*). Take some artificial berries and leaves, frosted to give a Christmas atmosphere, and cut them down into sprigs and secure them in the foam.

5 Finish off the design with tartan bows wired into place throughout the arrangement.

1

2

3

4

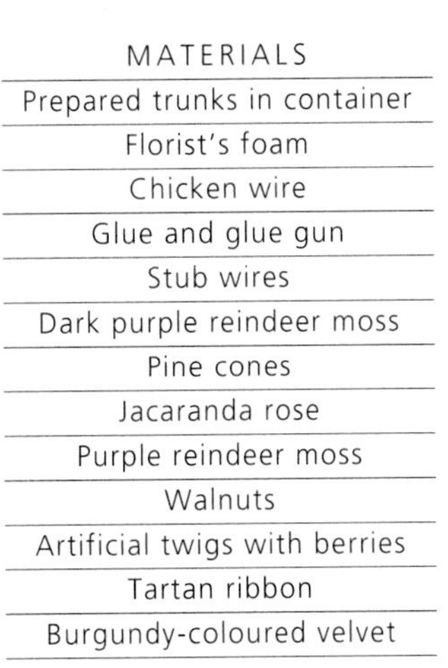

MATERIALS
Prepared trunks in container
Florist's foam
Chicken wire
Glue and glue gun
Stub wires
Dark purple reindeer moss
Pine cones
Jacaranda rose
Purple reindeer moss
Walnuts
Artificial twigs with berries
Tartan ribbon
Burgundy-coloured velvet

5

1

2

3

MATERIALS
Prepared trunk in terracotta flowerpot
Natural reindeer moss
Reel wire
Lichen-covered larch twigs
Cinnamon sticks
Tartan ribbon
Glue and glue gun
Stub wires
Christmas decorations
Panel pin and hammer

4

ADVANCED LEVEL

CHRISTMAS TWIG TREE

This larch twig tree is a substitute for the traditional pine Christmas tree. Either bedecked with gilded red apples and cinnamon sticks bundled together with tartan ribbon or left unadorned, it makes a wonderful focal point to a Christmas scene.

The lichen covering the larch twigs softens their stark appearance, and the small cones hint at the festive occasion. These are not the only materials you could use. Many types of pine or fir that don't drop their needles would also be appropriate. Once the trunk is secured in your container, it is a simple matter to bind the twig branches to it. The difficulty lies in positioning the twigs to that they splay out in a spiral, creating the overall shape.

1 Take a prepared trunk in a container (*see pp. 10-17*). Make sure that the trunk is long enough to reach the planned height of your finished tree. Cover the cement used to secure the trunk in the terracotta flowerpot with natural reindeer moss, glued into position with a glue gun. Attach one end of the reel wire to the trunk. Now take twigs of lichen-covered larch and slowly but firmly bind them on to the lower section of the tree trunk.

2 Continue in this fashion until you have constructed one complete tier of branches spiralling outward from the trunk.

3 Move up the trunk with the reel wire and create your second tier of branches around the tree trunk. Continue to work up the tree, binding on more and more tiers as you proceed.

4 When you reach the top of the trunk, nail a small panel pin in to act as an anchor for the last few branches. This will give a sharp point to the top of the tree. You may wish to leave the tree plain and enjoy it just as it is, or you could decorate it with tree lights fed up through the inside of the branches. You can also hang traditional Christmas decorations or make some fragrant ones out of cinnamon sticks tied with festive, tartan ribbon.

MATERIALS
Prepared block of florist's foam
Wheat
Stub wires
Natural raffia
Dried autumn leaves in various colours
Dried peppers
Dried baby corn on the cob
Dried fruit slices
Glue and glue gun

1

2

3

4

ADVANCED LEVEL

HARVEST SHEAF

Harvest is a celebration of nature – a rejoicing in the goodness of the sun ripening the fruits and crops of the countryside. This wheat sheaf is presented in traditional fashion and is evocative of the close of summer, when the long hot months mellow into cooler days and early dusks.

The red, rust, brown and orange hues of the dried leaves caught up in the raffia binding, alongside the sliced dried fruit, corn and bright peppers, produce an autumnal symphony. The technique involved in making this piece is not easy, and you should tackle it only after practising on some easier projects. For example, in the wheat and alchemilla arrangement (*see pp. 76-9*) a similar method of using bunched wheat is used. The illusion of an intact stem that is, in reality, two separate halves, is explored in the grouped basket project (*see pp. 24-5*).

Tackling these two projects first will help to build up your skill and confidence and ensure that when you attempt this sheaf you will succeed in making a first-class job of it.

1 Take a block of prepared florist's foam for a wall-mounted arrangement (*see pp. 10-17*). Gather some wheat into bunches, keeping the ears level. Wire their stems together with stub wires and twist the ends together. With this wire holding the lower section and your hand the upper, cut the top to the required size and secure it with another stub wire. Put the lower section to one side for later use. Take a prepared upper section and place it centrally in the top of the foam. Continue working from here, arranging more bunches into a fan. Position the bunches horizontally out of the foam about a third of the way down.

2 Arrange a shorter-stemmed fan close against the first. Leave enough space for a third fan, as shown.

3 Build up the third fan. Reduce the length of the stems, as you did the second fan. Fill in with bunches until the top is domed. Take some bottom sections and arrange them flat against the block. Start about 2in (5cm) lower than the dome. Continue until you reach the middle. Cut some shorter lengths, rewire them and push them into the base of the block, filling it completely. Now continue around the block with the longer stems until it is covered.

4 Form a second layer of long-stemmed bunches on top of the first. This time, arrange the stub wires in the 2in (5cm) of foam left free beneath the dome. Bend stub wires and push them through both bunches. Tie a thick bunch of raffia around the sheaf. Glue autumn leaves under the raffia. Wire dried peppers and baby corn to the sheaf and glue on slices of dried fruits.

INDEX

H

K L

M

N P

R

S

T

V

W

ACKNOWLEDGEMENTS

THE PUBLISHERS AND AUTHOR WOULD LIKE TO THANK THE FOLLOWING PEOPLE AND ORGANIZATIONS FOR THEIR GENEROUS HELP AND SUPPORT IN THE PRODUCTION OF THIS BOOK:

SUPPLIER OF ACCESSORIES AND PROPS

THE DINING ROOM SHOP
62-64 WHITE HART LANE
BARNES
LONDON SW13 OP2

SPECIAL THANKS TO

KATHIE GILL FOR INDEXING

CATE FOWLER FOR HER HELP WITH THE MANUSCRIPT

KIM CARTER AND ALAN DAVIS FOR THEIR TIME AND ASSISTANCE

LEONA SANDERS AND ANDREW JONES FOR TYPING AND PREPARARTION OF THE MANUSCRIPT

SANDRA AND PETER, NICK AND CAROLINE, AND JENNY AND STEWART FOR THE USE OF THEIR HOMES FOR PHOTOGRAPHY